How the Sweet Sound

THE MESSAGE OF
OUR BEST-LOVED HYMNS

RICHARD ALLEN FARMER

InterVarsity Press
Downers Grove, Illinois

InterVarsity Press
P.O. Box 1400, Downers Grove, IL 60515-1426
World Wide Web: www.ivpress.com
E-mail: mail@ivpress.com

InterVarsity Press® is the book-publishing division of InterVarsity Christian Fellowship/USA®, a student movement active on campus at hundreds of universities, colleges and schools of nursing in the United States of America, and a member movement of the International Fellowship of Evangelical Students. For information about local and regional activities, write Public Relations Dept., InterVarsity Christian Fellowship/USA, 6400 Schroeder Rd., P.O. Box 7895, Madison, WI 53707-7895, or visit the IVCF website at <www.ivcf.org>.

All Scripture quotations, unless otherwise indicated, are taken from the Holy Bible, New International Version®. NIV®. Copyright ©1973, 1978, 1984 by International Bible Society. Used by permission of Zondervan Publishing House. All rights reserved.

Design: Cindy Kiple

Images: Fototeca Storica Nazionale/Getty Images

ISBN 0-8308-3240-8

Printed in the United States of America ∞

Library of Congress Cataloging-in-Publication Data

Farmer, Richard Allen,
    How sweet the sound: the message of our best-loved hymns/Richard
Allen Farmer.
        p. cm.
    ISBN 0-8308-3240-8 (pbk.: alk. paper)
    1. Hymns, English—History and criticism. 2. Meditations. I.
Title.
BV310.F37 2004
264'.23—dc22

                                                                2003018832

P	18	17	16	15	14	13	12	11	10	9	8	7	6	5	4	3	2	1
Y	18	17	16	15	14	13	12	11	10	09	08	07	06	05	04	03		

Dedication

With profound gratitude, I dedicate this book to the congregation of the Trinity Baptist Church in the Bronx, New York. It was as a child in that vibrant gathering that I first heard hymns sung in memorable ways. The senior pastor, Dr. Nathaniel Tyler-Lloyd, came to this church in 1960 and went home to be with Jesus in 2002. In his distinguished pastoral ministry of nearly forty-two years, he insisted we sing an assortment of music. Hymns were not simply tolerated; they were treasured as part of our liturgical legacy.

Founded by middle-class African Americans in 1899, this body of believers continues to sing everything from Martin Luther to John Wesley to Andrae Crouch to John P. Kee. However, for them it is not an either-or dichotomy. To this day, I am comfortable in a wide variety of liturgical settings, from singing the chants in the Anglican tradition to enjoying the exuberant dancing of the saints at a Pentecostal church.

The singing of hymns is part of a well-spread table. I approached that table as a youngster and still feast on the ample food left there by the saints of old. Papa God be praised for such a rich heritage.

Contents

Introduction

We sang hymns at 808 East 224th Street, Bronx, New York, where the Trinity Baptist Church met and still meets today. Unless you were raised in a hymnless, contemporary expression of the historic Christian faith, you have probably sung a hymn or two yourself. Some of those hymns were so well known and well loved that we sang them frequently and enthusiastically. Others were set aside for seasonal use, dusted off in time for the Advent or Lenten season. Depending on the hymn in question and where I was in my spiritual pilgrimage, I found myself singing what I did not understand. Worship leaders compounded this problem by not always helping me understand what I sang. Though my home church did not have any song leaders, when I traveled to other churches I experienced worship leaders who waved their hands and encouraged us to "sing out." But I did not always understand what I was singing. As Philip asked the Ethiopian eunuch about his level of comprehension (Acts 8:30), so also we worship leaders ought to be asking congregations and small groups whether they understand what they are singing. I hope this book will help worshipers sing with their spirit and with their minds also (1 Corinthians 14:15).

I received my first Bible when I was twelve years old. Prior to that, if I wanted to look up a story that had been read in Sunday school class, I'd have to borrow my mother's Bible. When I received my very own Bible, I was delighted. I began to read it and know where things were. I got to the point where I knew my way around the book. As a budding musician who had started piano studies at the age of eleven, I wanted to get to know the hymnal as well as I was coming to know the Scriptures. The Bible and the hymnal became volumes I sought to master. Nearly forty years later, the romance goes on. I still seek to take a deeper look rather than a passing glance at Scripture and the hymnal. I want those two tomes to walk side by side and inform me. When I went to a Christ-centered college, I did not wave goodbye to either book. In chapel services we heard sermons and hymns. Rather than replace hymns with other styles of music, I saw hymns as the foundation upon which I built a musical house with appreciable diversity throughout. Today I am neither musically impoverished nor musically narrow. The sounds of hymns, jazz, gospel, ragtime, blues, baroque and rock have washed over me.

Why is it that we don't always relish the singing of hymns as we would a good novel or film? Are we dull of hearing? Bored? Ignorant? Musically illiterate or myopic? All of the above?

Allow me to take you on a journey that invites a recovery or discovery of a legacy that we ignore to our shame and peril. Permit me to suggest that the problem with hymns, if there is one, is not that they are dull pieces of music; it is that we rarely hear them sung well. If you have come from a tradition in which you have heard "Immortal, Invisible, God Only Wise" sung with confident thunder, blessed are you. If you think all hymns are dry, irrelevant and will induce sleep, impoverished are you. Perhaps as a result of reading this book you will come away believing there is hope for this third millennium expression of the lovers of God in Christ.

In this book, I will explore twenty-five hymns, taking and dissecting a few lines from each hymn so that we may rejoice in the richness of the text. Some hymns raise questions that the thinking singer must answer. I will unpack the theological problems and questions posed by some texts. Other texts call for celebration, and I will simply get the party started by lifting up the richness of a well-turned phrase or a well-stated thought.

This book is neither exhaustive nor ultimate. If we are people committed to regularly flossing our brains, we are always thinking about what we're singing. This book is merely a discussion starter. I give thanks that we have some writers, who in the last five years, have given the church some extraordinary pieces of music. I want us to enjoy this music; I also want the church to enjoy those pieces that were written before 1900. Why must we choose one over the other? Why can we not appreciate the fact that Papa God has spoken in centuries past and continues to speak in these days? Not all significant composers are dead. Neither do they all live in Nashville.

SECTION 1

About
God

Come, Thou Fount of Every Blessing

INVITING GOD IN

1. *Come, Thou Fount of every blessing,*
   Tune my heart to sing Thy grace;
   Streams of mercy, never ceasing,
   Call for songs of loudest praise.
   Teach me some melodious sonnet,
   Sung by flaming tongues above.
   Praise the mount—I'm fixed upon it—
   Mount of Thy redeeming love.

2. *Here I raise my Ebenezer;*
   Hither by Thy help I'm come;
   And I hope, by Thy good pleasure,
   Safely to arrive at home.
   Jesus sought me when a stranger,
   Wandering from the fold of God;
   He, to rescue me from danger,
   Interposed His precious blood.

3. *O to grace how great a debtor*
   Daily I'm constrained to be!
   Let thy goodness, like a fetter,
   Bind my wandering heart to Thee.
   Prone to wander, Lord, I feel it,
   Prone to leave the God I love;
   Here's my heart, o take and seal it;
   Seal it for Thy courts above.

ROBERT ROBINSON, CIRCA 1758

$\mathcal{I}$ sang this hymn for years without fully understanding the full import of its text. It opens with an invocation: "Come, Thou Fount of every blessing," who is, of course, God himself. But do we really have to ask God to come? Isn't it assumed that he is already in every place? We read in the Psalms,

> *Where can I go from your Spirit?*
> *Where can I flee from your presence?*
> *If I go up to the heavens, you are there;*
> *if I make my bed in the depths, you are there.*
> *If I rise on the wings of the dawn,*
> *if I settle on the far side of the sea,*
> *even there your hand will guide me,*
> *your right hand will hold me fast. (Psalm 139:7-10)*

If this is true, and it is, why sing any song that begins with "come"? The Lord already inhabits every nook and cranny of the earth. Perhaps we should never, verbally or musically, offer an invocation. Maybe there is no need to invoke God's presence. After all, to do so would nullify our belief in his omnipresence. In the African American church, sometimes deacons in prayer ask God to "stop by here a little while," or to "stop by the hospital and look on Sister Jones." I always thought this was a bit unnecessary, since God knew we had gathered in his name. He also knew the whereabouts and the needs of Sister Jones. However, I now understand this differently. When we sing or verbalize an invocation, we do not so much *invite* as we *affirm* the presence of God.

This hymn, written when Robert Robinson was twenty-three years old, is not so much an invitation for God to show up as it is an invitation for him to do a specific work.

As a trained pianist, I find an out-of-tune instrument to be of little use and unpleasant to play. I want the piano to respond to my touch, and in order for that to happen, it has to be in tune. When we sing anything that begins with "come," it is an invitation for God to tune our hearts to sing his grace. There is no debate as to whether or not God is among us. There is, however, great concern that as he moves within and upon his people, we might not invite him to do his wondrous work in us. So we sing "come." Another hymn, "Come, Thou Almighty King," echoes this thought in similar language:

> **Come**, *Thou Almighty King,*
> *Help us Thy name to sing,*
> *Help us to praise:*
> *Father all glorious,*
> *O'er all victorious,*
> **Come**, *and reign over us,*
> *Ancient of Days.*
>
> Anonymous, circa 1757 (*Emphasis mine*)

Whenever we sing hymns that invite God in, we are not suggesting that he is not already present. We are aware, however, that we are not always in the proper frame of mind for significant worship. When I was a pastor of a local church, I frequently asked the organist not to play the prelude while people were entering the sanctuary since it was background music and people hardly paid attention to it. Instead, I would call the gathering to order and then invite the congregation to hear the prelude and to use those moments to ask God to tune them up so we could experience true worship together.

The second stanza of "Come, Thou Fount of Every Blessing" interests me the most even though I sang it for years without any knowledge of what "my Ebenezer" meant. The concept of Ebenezer is drawn from 1 Samuel 7, where the Israelites and Philistines were battling against each other. Israel, as was often the case, was outnumbered and, humanly speaking, stood no chance of being victorious. Israel was afraid of the Philistines (1 Samuel 7:7). The trembling people of God asked their leader, the prophet Samuel, to storm the gates of heaven on their behalf. Samuel prepared an offering and offered it to the Lord, accompanied by earnest prayer. The Lord answered Samuel and gave Israel the victory over the Philistines. We read: "Then Samuel took a stone and set it up between Mizpah and Shen. He named it Ebenezer, saying, 'Thus far has the LORD helped us'" (1 Samuel 7:12).

To raise an Ebenezer is to set up a visible reminder of the Lord God's faithfulness to you in your battles. Perhaps it is a framed certificate saying you completed a college degree that was especially difficult for you. Perhaps you have an entry in your journal, which is no more than a detailed account of a specific habit God enabled you to overcome. Every time you read that dog-eared page, it's an Ebenezer moment—you are reminded that the Lord helped you. While we often pride ourselves on having a keen ability to retain information, our minds usually cannot remember everything. We are far better off having some physical reminders of God's faithfulness to us.

In this regard, I am doing my best to take advantage of the technology available to us today. My camera automatically prints on the back of the photo the date on which it was taken. Frequently, to help me remember I also add a few lines on the back of the photo to describe who was in the picture and what the occasion was. I am not advocating idolatry or sentimentalism here. I am not suggesting you take a rock and give it a prominent place in your house, bowing before it each time you pass by. I am, however, suggesting that some items may serve to stimulate your memory of a mighty act of God. Inasmuch as that article might provoke your praise of the eternal God, it is a good thing.

I am a first generation college student. In my memory, there were no members of my immediate family who graduated from college.

When I look at my diploma, it reminds me of God's grace in allowing me that life-changing experience. For you, the Ebenezer might be an envelope with a deed to your house in it. "Paid" is written across the face of the envelope, and you are reminded of how God allowed you to pay off that house. For others, Ebenezer is a certain place to which they return annually to be reminded of what God did there. The purpose of the Ebenezer is to rekindle the sacred flame of memory so that God might be praised.

The raising of the Ebenezer is impossible for the allegedly self-made person. Such a person can never say, "thus far the Lord has helped me," because that person doesn't believe God has helped at all. Some are naive enough to think that what they have accomplished, they have accomplished on their own. In one of the Bible's most humbling phrases, Jesus says, "Apart from me, you can do nothing" (John 15:5). Spiritual maturity presupposes our acknowledgment of the direct activity of God in our lives. We raise our Ebenezers—monuments to the help of God—so that we are spared the temptation to raise monuments to ourselves.

In the last stanza of "Come, Thou Fount of Every Blessing," we sing "prone to wander, Lord I feel it." Whenever I sing that line I want to shake my fist and declare that I shall never wander from the fold, from the faith, from my commitment to Jesus. But in my more honest moments, I know I am not above the temptation. Thanks be to God that he holds us.

The story is told that the author of this hymn was riding in a stagecoach and heard a woman humming a tune. The woman asked Robert Robinson what he thought of the hymn she was humming. Robinson allegedly said, "Madam, I am the poor unhappy man who wrote that hymn many years ago, and I would give a thousand worlds, if I had them, to enjoy the feeling I had then."[1] Yes, even the writer of a great text can wander from its power. May we never stop saying to God, "Come, tune my heart."

2

A Mighty Fortress Is Our God

A CELEBRATION

OF STRENGTH

1. A mighty fortress is our God,
   A bulwark never failing;
   Our helper He amid the flood
   Of mortal ills prevailing.
   For still our ancient foe
   Doth seek to work us woe;
   His craft and power are great,
   And armed with cruel hate,
   On earth is not His equal.

2. Did we in our own strength confide,
   Our striving would be losing,
   Were not the right Man on our side,
   The Man of God's own choosing.
   Dost ask who that may be?
   Christ Jesus, it is He;
   Lord Sabbaoth, his name,
   From age to age the same,
   And He must win the battle.

3. And though this world, with devils filled,
   Should threaten to undo us,
   We will not fear, for God hath willed
   His truth to triumph through us.
   The prince of darkness grim—
   We tremble not for him;
   His rage we can endure,
   For lo, his doom is sure;
   One little word shall fell him.

4. *That word above all earthly powers—*
   No thanks to them—abideth;
   The Spirit and the gifts are ours
   Through him who with us sideth.
   Let goods and kindred go,
   This mortal life also;
   The body they may kill;
   God's truth abideth still,
   His kingdom is forever.

MARTIN LUTHER, 1529

$\mathcal{I}$ was a seventh grade student when I heard this song for the first time in my choral music class. I remember asking my teacher, Miss Isabel Berg, what a bulwark was. She described it as something very strong that you can't get around. To this day, that definition satisfies me—our God is a God of strength. No wimpy, impotent God have we. This hymn is based on Psalm 46:1-2:

> God is our refuge and strength,
> an ever-present help in trouble.
> Therefore we will not fear, though the earth give way
> and the mountains fall into the heart of the sea.

Frederick the Great described this hymn as "God Almighty's Grenadier March," Scottish theologian Dr. James Moffatt referred to it as "the greatest hymn of the greatest man in the greatest period of German history," and others call it "The Battle Hymn of the Reformation." In that most difficult of periods for the church—the Reformation—Christians needed to be reminded to stand firm in their faith. It was not a time for spiritual cowards. Luther often used his music to confront and to comfort. In April 1521 Luther appeared before the Diet of Worms (*Diet* refers to an assembly; *Worms* was a city in Germany) to be questioned about his writings and confrontational statements regarding the Roman Catholic clergy and the papacy. Luther stood tall before Charles V and other dignitaries as he made it clear that he intended to obey God rather than the king or the pope. "A Mighty Fortress Is Our God" was written shortly after this incident and soon became a battle cry and a word of hope for the protesters. In fact, those who followed Luther in their stance were called the "protestant ones," from which is derived the word *Protestant*. The four stanzas of this hymn provide a clear exposition of the doctrine of spiritual warfare. Those forces both human and demonic must step back when our mighty God rises.

In the first stanza, Luther celebrates God's strength. It matters much that God is strong; if he is not, our faith is useless. If we are prey to every other deity who challenges our allegiance to the living God, what is the point of serving him? Our confidence is that we are preserved and sustained by this God. While we celebrate our strong God, says Luther, let us acknowledge our common enemy. Our "ancient foe" is as committed to evangelism as God is. The devil is crafty and powerful and no one like him exists in the earth. Luther will say that to go against Satan and win, one would be foolish to go in one's own strength. Enter, Jesus the Christ. The Christ does not merely win many of his skirmishes. He is not simply an adequate fighter. He goes into direct battle with Satan, and Christ is victorious. No matter what happens, the church can rest in this great truth—God protects his people and they shall be more than conquerors (Romans 8:35-37). For Martin Luther and other reformers, there was no greater comfort and assurance than the concept of a personal God who speaks through the Bible. They stood defiantly on the authority of God's Word. Willing to die for their faith if necessary, they cited the motto: "By Grace alone (*sola gratia*), through Faith alone (*sola fide*), according to Scripture alone (*sola Scriptura*), for God's Glory alone (*soli Deo gloria*)."

In the second stanza, Luther issues a warning clothed in an admonition. If we were to confide in our own strength, "our striving would be losing." If we were foolish enough to engage in spiritual warfare through mere human cleverness, such effort would be futile. We need the right person on our side. Jesus the Christ is the person God chose for us. Backed by such a chosen one, we can function without fear.

The third stanza says that even if the world was filled with devils, we should not fear—God has already worked out the details of our warfare. He has willed his truth to triumph through us. Because of this truth, we need not tremble. Anxiety and confidence dare not try to coexist in the same person. If we trust this God, we will not tremble for fear of the devil. If we tremble in fear, it indicates our lack of trust in this God.

We have frequent thunderstorms in Texas. As a toddler, my son seemed to look forward to thunderstorms because he went to a designated safe closet away from the outside walls of our house. Whenever he heard thunder, he loved running into that closet. My wife and I had assured him that in that safe place he would hardly even hear the thunder. Similarly, God has provided us with a refuge from the rumblings of the prince of darkness. We enter the refuge that is Jesus and we hardly even hear the devil's threats. We can endure his rage, says Luther, because of the pronouncements of our God. One little word from God shall topple our enemy.

In the fourth stanza, Luther assures us that the word of God stands, no thanks to our foes. Luther almost suggests a stripping down of the temporal life in order that we might fully appreciate the more worthy and weighty spiritual life. He bids us let goods and people go. He suggests that we put the mortal (physical) life in its proper perspective. All of these are disposable. Our hearts are not. Our God is not. Let our enemies, says Martin Luther, destroy our bodies. We would still have stood upon an unchanging and indestructible word from God. Hebrews 12:27 speaks of things that can be shaken and things that cannot be. Luther would say that we, the people of God, cannot be shaken. We are steadfast because God is even more so. His kingdom is forever and that unwavering commitment to permanence on the part of our God is what encourages his followers.

In the preface to his Wittenberg Hymnal of 1524, Luther wrote:

That it is good and God pleasing to sing hymns is, I think, known to every Christian; for everyone is aware not only of the example of the prophets and kings in the Old Testament who praised God with song and sound, with poetry and psaltery, but also of the common and ancient custom of the Christian Church to sing Psalms. . . . Like Moses in his song (Exodus 15:2), we may now boast that Christ is our praise and song.

Can you picture Luther and his colleagues singing songs to God and about God and having those songs become their fighting songs? Knowing the background of this hymn may give us suggestions about how we can sing it. This is one song I would not want to hear sung to a swing beat. It is a militant song designed to inspire and motivate the people of God as they faced their foe. It's not a ditty or a show tune. Some years ago, I was the speaker at a denominational conference. The planners were not theologically conservative and wondered what I might say. I preached a series of sermons on word pictures of the believer in the Scripture. Each night I said that we were the salt of the earth and the light of the world. I told the planners that one evening I would use a military metaphor to suggest that we were all soldiers. They objected strongly, citing our need to be pacifists in this violent world. The reminder that violence is seemingly ruling the day is a good one, but there is no escaping our spiritual militancy. Martin Luther knew he was in a battle. Let us not soften the language in order to appease a crowd that wants to make friends with this present age.

So here we stand, more than four hundred years after Luther's battle cry. We find ourselves reminded of the greatness of our God. This God *has* won the battle, and he *must* win the battles that are yet to come.

3

Immortal, Invisible, God Only Wise

A FOCUSED
VIEW OF GOD

1. *Immortal, invisible, God only wise,*
   In light inaccessible hid from our eyes,
   Most blessed, most glorious, the Ancient of Days
   Almighty, victorious, Thy great name we praise.

2. *Unsetting, unhasting, and silent as light,*
   Nor wanting, nor wasting, Thou rulest in might;
   Thy justice, like mountains, high soaring above
   Thy clouds, which are fountains of goodness and love.

3. *To all, life Thou givest, to both great and small,*
   In all life Thou livest, the true life of all.
   We blossom and flourish as leaves on the tree,
   And wither and perish—but naught changeth Thee.

4. *Great Father of glory, pure Father of light,*
   Thine angels adore Thee, all veiling their sight;
   All praise we would render; O help us to see
   'Tis only the splendor of light hideth Thee!

Walter C. Smith, 1867

$\mathcal{D}$uring the Alaska Christian Ministries Convention, I held a seminar on worship. A participant asked me what the definition of a hymn was. I told her that such a definition is somewhat elusive, since songs we call gospel songs are also included in hymnals and not all hymns necessarily measure up to a tight definition. Then I told her that a hymn is a piece of music that speaks of God and his character, rather than speaking about God and what he has done for an individual. While there are many exceptions on either side of that working definition, allow me to offer it for our consideration here. Smith's hymn is written as if he dared not speak of humans; he only wanted to describe God. We turn to Paul's first letter to his son in the faith, Timothy, to find the biblical inspiration for this hymn. Paul is so excited about God's grace that he breaks into a doxology: "Now to the King eternal, immortal, invisible, the only God, be honor and glory for ever and ever. Amen" (1 Timothy 1:17). However, there is a particularly significant word in this Scripture that does not appear in the hymn title. Let's dissect this Scripture and see what wondrous things we are saying about God when we sing this hymn.

God is king. The word *king* appears in 1 Timothy 1:17, but not in the title of the hymn. To say God is king is to acknowledge the supremacy of God. To say God is king is to say he reigns over his created order. A king may be benign, passive, weak and a mere figurehead, which God is not. A king may also be violent, self-serving, malevolent and abusive, which God is not. A king may also establish laws, give his subjects the freedom to obey them and thus prosper, or allow the citizens to disobey the laws and live with the consequences, which God has done. Some suggest that God cannot be sovereign and humanity be truly free at the same time, because a sovereign God would stop his creation from destroying itself, even if that creation were given free will. A good and sovereign God, some say, would not let humanity get into such a mess. To say God is king is to articulate a doctrine that cannot be fully explained. That God is king is well substantiated in Scripture (Psalm 96:10; 97:1; 99:1; 135:6; 145:11-13; Jeremiah 10:10; 1 Timothy 6:15). That humanity is free to choose is also substantiated in the Scriptures (Exodus 15:26; Deuteronomy 15:4; Job 36:11; Colossians 1:22-23). The king stands ready to rule over his creation. If he finds no resistance in us, blessings accrue as we cooperate with his reign. If we say we shall have no king rule over us, we forfeit many blessings.

The king is eternal. This means both that the king is everlasting and that he is the king of all ages. As we sing this hymn we celebrate the truth that God shall always be. We also rejoice that he is the God of the past, the present and the future. Throughout the Old Testament we read of kings who reigned for many years then rested with their fathers (2 Chronicles 21:1). We will never read that of God; he reigns forever and ever.

The eternal king is immortal. In our parlance, *eternal* and *immortal* are interchangeable. We speak of something as lasting forever (eternal) and as not being bound to the mortal (immortal). But when we use those words to refer to God, we are saying two very different things. To say God is king eternal is to say he reigns in every era. He was and is and shall be. To say he is immortal is to say he is imperishable. He cannot be destroyed. Time never creeps up on him. He is not bound by clocks or calendars at all. The indictment upon some people in Romans was that they exchanged the glory of the immortal God for perishable images (Romans 1:23). To put it in today's language, they traded him who lasts forever for a perishable product with an expiration date. First Timothy 6:16 says that our Lord God is the only being who has the quality of immortality. The rest of us will put on immortality, but we do not possess it as part of our original created character.

The eternal, immortal king is invisible. In 1 Timothy 6:16, we read a supplement to 1:17—God lives in unapproachable light and no one has seen him. The closest we get to seeing God is to see his glory. His glory is ultimately, and most clearly, seen in his Son, the Lord Christ (John 1:14, 18), who is the "image of the invisible God" (Colossians 1:15). If you long to see God, look at Christ, for all that God is, he has placed in Jesus.

On one occasion Jesus was chatting with his disciples. His words were dripping with finality and his departure was imminent. Philip thought that if he and the others could get a peek of the heavenlies that might suffice until they saw Jesus again. Philip simply asked for Jesus to show them the Father. Jesus, surely with disappointment, said, "Don't you know me, Philip, even after I have been among you such a long time? Anyone who has seen me has seen the Father. How can you say, 'Show us the Father'? Don't you believe that I am in the Father, and that the Father is in me?" (John 14:9-10). The invisible God has made himself most visible in his Son. To say God is invisible, however, does not mean that he cannot be seen. It merely means that he is not seen. He has chosen not to make himself visible. Perhaps he knew we would be overwhelmed by his radiance. In Exodus 33, Moses begs to see God in all his effulgence (Exodus 33:18). But God tells Moses that Moses will only get to see God's goodness and a manifestation of God's presence. "'But,' he said, 'you cannot see my face, for no one may see me and live'" (Exodus 33:20). This king retains the right to not show himself in all the ways he could, in order that in his invisibility, his people may truly, in faith, see him.

The eternal, immortal, invisible king is unique. Most Bible translations do not have the word *wise* in 1 Timothy 1:17. God is the only God. God is in a classification by himself and has no peers. As we sing this hymn, we resist the temptation to speak of the eternal, immortal, invisible king as if he is one of a host of equal gods. No, this God is the only God. Let him speak for himself through his prophet, Isaiah:

For this is what the LORD says—
he who created the heavens,
   he is God. . . .
"I am the LORD, and there is no other." (Isaiah 45:18)

If a hymn is a song that tells us what God is like, then the hymn "Immortal, Invisible, God Only Wise" is one that adheres most strictly to the definition. It describes God's character and ways. He is, according to Walter C. Smith, "unsetting, unhasting, and silent as light." He displays neither want nor decay. He gives life to all. He never changes. He is pure glory and light. And, as if that isn't glorious enough, this same God has invited us into union with him through Christ.

4

Guide Me, O Thou Great Jehovah

A PILGRIM'S PLEA

1. Guide me, O Thou great Jehovah,
   Pilgrim through this barren land.
   I am weak, but Thou art mighty;
   Hold me with Thy powerful hand.
   Bread of heaven, bread of heaven,
   Feed me till I want no more;
   Feed me till I want no more.

2. Open now the crystal fountain,
   Whence the healing stream doth flow;
   Let the fire and cloudy pillar
   Lead me all my journey through;
   Strong deliverer, strong deliverer,
   Be Thou still my strength and shield;
   Be Thou still my strength and shield.

3. When I tread the verge of Jordan,
   Bid my anxious fears subside;
   Bear me through the swelling current,
   Land me safe on Canaan's side.
   Songs of praises, songs of praises,
   I will ever give to Thee;
   I will ever give to Thee.

WILLIAM WILLIAMS, 1745
ENGLISH TRANSLATION BY PETER WILLIAMS

On one occasion, Jesus took pity on a group of people because they seemed to be leaderless (Matthew 9:36). In Jesus' mind, if you have no guide, you are to be pitied. By the way, when we call on this God for guidance, we may call him God, Lord, Jehovah (a translation of *Yahweh*, the Hebrew name for God) or Rock of Ages. He has multiple names. I am so glad, for I would not want my prayers to go unanswered simply because I used "God" instead of "Jehovah."

What difference does it make that we are a guided people? Guides keep us from going astray and secure our direction by their knowledge of the path. My friend Dick Rohrer is a hunting guide in Kodiak, Alaska. Clients pay him not because he can guarantee them a Kodiak bear on their hunt (he cannot), but because he knows the way. He knows the path and he knows the bears. While there is a strong possibility that clients will bag a big one, they pay for Dick's knowledge more than anything else. To say God is our guide is to affirm his perfect knowledge and our need of it. There are at least three ways in which God guides us.

God guides us by his written Word. Such clear wisdom is contained in the Bible, that whoever neglects it does so at one's own peril. Recently I was preaching to a group of students at a Christian university and celebrated aloud with them, that every eighth verse of Psalm 119 is a celebration of the Word of God. Using a host of synonyms to frame his praise, the psalmist speaks of the joy he experiences when he reads the law, statutes, commands, teachings, decrees and precepts. At the risk of sounding trite, let me suggest that we will find guidance if we would read the Bible. In it there are words that enable sound decision-making. In Psalm 119, we read that the unfolding of God's Word gives light; it gives understanding to the simple (Psalm 119:130).

However, one can take this idea of biblical guidance to an extreme. One can start hunting through the pages of the Bible in order to find a verse to justify some desire, thus making one's action "of God." Given enough time and enough warped creativity, I can make the Bible say anything I want it to. If I desperately want that new boat, I merely claim Psalm 37:4:

> Delight yourself in the LORD,
>   and he will give you the desires of your heart.

I then simply assure myself that I am delighting in the Lord. He is then obligated to get me the boat, which is the desire of my heart. If I want to murder someone, I simply quote Jeremiah 18:21:

> Let their wives be made childless and widows;
>   let their men be put to death.

Apart from their contexts, both Psalm 37:4 and Jeremiah 18:21 can be misunderstood. As we delight ourselves in our Lord God, he conforms us in such a way that his will becomes ours. We begin to want what he wants. The desires of our God's heart become the desires of our hearts. Likewise, when Jeremiah utters his words, he is calling for a specific response from God to what his enemies have done. Jeremiah wants God to even the score. The verse does not serve as a murderer's motto.

Manipulation of the Word of God is all too common. When we ask God to guide us, we presuppose a submission to this guiding God, rather than a manufacturing of some circumstance into which we then tell others we were led. How does God guide us by his Word? Does the Bible actually speak? Yes, if we can think a bit mystically. Rather than waiting for voices to be heard as we read, let us expect that God addresses our inner person as we read. The Bible is replete with promises—let's claim them. It is packed with commandments— let's obey them. It is full of accounts of God's action in history—let's appreciate what God has done. The Bible contains stories of women and men who faithfully obeyed God—let's imitate them. We also read of people who failed to follow God—let us avoid their example. As we read, there are many places where we can identify with the text. It is an unwavering commitment on the reader's part to allow the words from the Bible to influence our thoughts about God and about life that constitutes biblical guidance.

God guides us through the counsel of others. This is very exciting but also very scary since we can allow others to play God in our lives. It is true that "a wise man listens to advice" (Proverbs 12:15).

But we do not help ourselves if the person we listen to is also a fool. However, when we seek counsel from wise people, God often uses them to speak truth to us. God may choose to deliver his message for us through our friends. Suppose I am trying to decide between two job offers, both of which are commensurate with my skills, training and qualifications. Since the Bible does not address specific job offers, I might look outside the Bible for some guidance. A friend who knows me very well might say, "Richard, in job 'A' you could maximize your impact on others. In scenario 'B' you'll be comfortable but not especially useful." I want to receive that word from my friend with great seriousness. God may be using my friend's knowledge of me and my openness to this counsel to reach me.

God may guide us through circumstances. I want to be extremely cautious here because this is an area where subjectivism could rule the day. Any one event can be interpreted for both good and evil. The half-filled glass of chocolate milk can be described as both half full and half empty. Both descriptions would be correct. When things happen to us, how ought we to interpret them?

Every circumstance will point us to a biblical principle. The maturity and biblical literacy of the believer will determine how quickly that biblical principle is discovered. For every event there will be a pointing to a truth. For instance, if a friend is incarcerated for burglary and I go to visit this person, that circumstance leads me to some thinking about what it means to live in community, the nature of civil behavior and what I think about my neighbor. The visit to the prison is a circumstance which prompts my thinking about theological truth. If I am fully alert, God's truth can be driven home in my life through a prison visit to my friend. In that case, God has used a specific circumstance to instruct and remind me.

Sometimes the lesson is much subtler. It might be that as I am walking across a boulevard I am grazed by a passing car. That event may lead me to think about how God protects his people, the randomness of car accidents, the fragile nature of life or the need to provide for my family in the event of my sudden death. I maintain that the question for us to answer is not "Does God speak to his people?" Rather, it is "Do I hear God when he speaks?" He can be quite arresting in the seemingly mundane. There he reminds us of something we have known but needed to think of again. Often, Jehovah guides this pilgrim in daily events. In the hymn "This Is My Father's World" there is a line that says as much: "In the rustling grass I hear him pass; he speaks to me everywhere."

Why would we sing "Guide Me, O Thou Great Jehovah" unless we saw ourselves as those in need of guidance? The writer, William Williams, sees us as pilgrims who are in need of and in search of a home. It is critical that we do not define ourselves as earthbound but as pilgrims. The earthbound are too at home here already and have no need of Jehovah's guidance. It is the pilgrim, aware of inner weaknesses, who cries out to this delivering God. When Israel wandered through the desert, toward the Red Sea, the Lord led them: "By day the Lord went ahead of them in a pillar of cloud to guide them on their way and by night in a pillar of fire to give them light, so that they could travel by day or night" (Exodus 13:21).

While we do not experience the clouds and the fire in visible ways most of the time, we have this same leading God as our God. He still provides guidance for those weak pilgrims who are unashamed to confess their weaknesses and who are unafraid to call on him. He still feeds those who want the bread of heaven. He still bears, through the swelling current of death, those who trust in him.

5

How Firm a Foundation

GOODBYE
TO QUICKSAND

1. How firm a foundation, ye saints of the Lord,
   Is laid for your faith in His excellent Word!
   What more can He say than to you He hath said,
   To you who for refuge to Jesus have fled?

2. "Fear not, I am with thee; O be not dismayed,
   For I am thy God, I will still give thee aid;
   I'll strengthen thee, help thee, and cause thee to stand,
   Upheld by My righteous, omnipotent hand."

3. "When through fiery trials thy pathway shall lie,
   My grace, all-sufficient, shall be thy supply;
   The flame shall not hurt thee; I only design
   Thy dross to consume and thy gold to refine."

4. "The soul that on Jesus hath leaned for repose,
   I will not, I will not desert to his foes;
   That soul, though all hell should endeavor to shake,
   I'll never, no never, no never forsake!"

RIPPON'S "SELECTION OF HYMNS," 1787

A few years ago, my wife, Rosemary, and I had a house built for us. It was exciting to visit the construction site almost daily and watch the workers. Often we'd visit the site after working hours and walk the lot when no one was there. On one such walk, after the foundation had been poured, Rosemary wondered aloud how such a large house could fit on such a small foundation. I assured her that the builders knew what they were doing and that she could not look at the mere foundation and determine how the house would fit. When the remainder of the house was built shortly thereafter, Rosemary saw the big picture.

In ways too wonderful for us to fully comprehend, the faith of the lovers of Christ looks inadequate to sustain the superstructure. Yet here we are celebrating stability in the midst of a culture of quicksand and overwhelming floodwaters. Paul wrote to the church at Corinth, "For no one can lay any foundation other than the one already laid, which is Jesus Christ. If any man builds on this foundation using gold, silver, costly stones, wood, hay or straw, his work will be shown for what it is, because the Day will bring it to light" (1 Corinthians 3:11-13).

What gave stability to our house and what gives constancy to our faith is the foundation. For our faith, that foundation is the collected utterances of God, written by faithful, inspired writers.

The first stanza of this hymn clearly says that those who have fled to Jesus for refuge need not clamor for another word. Knowing we are stabilized by and through his Word, we need not fear. To sing a hymn such as this is not to suggest that we who sing it have no fear. In the hymn we affirm our great God and the fortitude he gives to those who follow him. We are not people who clutch a crutch, hoping this "religion thing" works out. No, we have a firm footing. How does one arrive at such a place? Is it a matter of positive thinking, self-affirming statements and good thoughts? No. The reason we can be so secure in our spiritual footing is that God has spoken. The hymn asks, "What more can he say than to you he has said?" That is an excellent question. If Papa God has said he will sustain us, what more can he say? He who has spoken in the Scripture, and ultimately in the sending of his Son, is reliable.

Reynolds Lloyd English Sr. (1902-1988) was my maternal grandfather. Of the many traits I admired in Pop was his reliability. If he said he would do something, he would do it. He came to my recitals at Town Hall when I was a developing pianist. He came to my college graduation. He would help you out if you were in a mess, with anything from dollars to mechanical help. You could accept his word as good. Our God is greater than Pop English. How dare we trust mere mortals, yet doubt this glorious God. What more can he say?

In this hymn, stanzas two through four have God speaking. Did you hear the promises?

- I am with thee.
- I will give thee aid.
- I'll strengthen thee.
- I'll cause thee to stand.
- My grace will be a sufficient supply for you.
- The flame shall not hurt you.
- I have designed experiences for you to refine you.
- I will not desert or forsake you as you face your foes.

If ever a human spoke these words to me, I'd be ecstatic. Yet sometimes when I hear this hymn sung, I wonder if we really believe God is speaking. If we did, we'd sing it differently. That is, we'd sing with passion and audible conviction. I recently took the time to read again the opening of the Declaration of Independence. In the second paragraph we read of "certain inalienable Rights . . . Life, Liberty and the pursuit of Happiness." Many would go to great lengths to protect these rights. According to the founders of our country, the source of such rights is the Creator. But today many want political independence and life, liberty and their pursuits apart from their Creator.

Similarly, this hymn does not suggest a nebulous standing on "something." We stand in Someone. As unrealistic as a search for freedom is apart from freedom's source, so is a search for a foundation apart from stability's source. The old building at my home church in the Bronx, New York, had wooden floors. The entrance was on the ground level, and the sanctuary was on the second floor of the simple building. So, when you entered the building, you very often heard toes tapping above your head. As the saints sang, they tapped their feet, and it shook the floor beneath them. I can still remember them declaring, with rhythmic feet, the lines from another classic hymn, "On Christ the solid rock I stand. All other ground is sinking sand. All other ground is sinking sand." They declared that God was our foundation.

Attributed to several different artists, a story is told of a young painter who presented his work to an older, more experienced artist. The mature artist examined the portrait of Christ for some time. He then said to the young artist, "You don't love him." The young man was a bit startled, whereupon the master artist said, "If you loved him, you'd paint him better."

If we really understood what this hymn writer is saying, we would sing it better. We would sing as if Papa God himself is speaking, reminding us not to be afraid. It is because no matter how small it appears to us as we walk around the site, we have a firm foundation.

6

Holy, Holy, Holy

A GOD LIKE NO OTHER

1. *Holy, holy, holy!*
   Lord God Almighty!
   Early in the morning our song shall rise to Thee;
   Holy, holy, holy!
   Merciful and mighty!
   God in three Persons, blessed Trinity!

2. *Holy, holy, holy!*
   All the saints adore thee,
   Casting down their golden crowns around the glassy sea;
   Cherubim and seraphim falling down before Thee,
   Which wert, and art, and evermore shalt be.

3. *Holy, holy, holy!*
   Tho' the darkness hide Thee,
   Tho' the eye of sinful man thy glory may not see,
   Only Thou art holy; there is none beside Thee
   Perfect in power, in love, and purity.

4. *Holy, holy, holy!*
   Lord God Almighty!
   All Thy works shall praise Thy name,
   in earth, and sky, and sea;
   Holy, holy, holy!
   Merciful and Mighty!
   God in three Persons, blessed Trinity!

REGINALD HEBER, 1826

$\mathcal{I}$f one of the differences between a hymn and a gospel song is that the hymn speaks of and to God more than of or to human experience, this hymn is outstanding. It speaks of God's character and is filled with adoration. It was written for Trinity Sunday, that day set aside to celebrate the Holy Trinity. It is always celebrated on the Sunday following Pentecost, which is fifty days after Resurrection Day (Easter). There is evidence that Trinity Sunday was observed as far back as the tenth century. In 1334 Pope John XXII approved the celebration for the entire church.

While many do not think deeply about the Trinity and the complex nature of the eternal God, this is a crucial concept. If Christ is not God, we are without hope. A merely good man with prophetic tendencies would be incapable of saving us. I find Heber's text interesting, because although it is a hymn in praise of the Trinity, he does not give us an exposition of the Trinity. This hymn does not devote a separate stanza to the Father, the Son and the Holy Spirit, a logical format from my perspective. Instead, Heber keeps our focus on God the Father and describes him in terms most memorable.

In stanza one, God is praised for his mercy and might. What a wedding of terms, which could appear in opposition. Romans 11:22 speaks of the "kindness and sternness of God." Those terms don't seem to go together. Yet when one speaks of God, those terms are perfectly blended. He is the God of love and judgment. He is the Lion and Lamb. He is a disciplining father and a tender mother. He is merciful and mighty. We have all experienced people in whom one of those attributes is dominant. We have never seen them in perfect tension except in our God.

In stanza two we are invited to join others who also find God worthy of our worship. We are urged to fall down with the cherubim and

seraphim. Both were celestial beings, with seraphim being mentioned only in Isaiah 6. Cherubim are mentioned in the Bible as those
creatures who are assigned to guard the Garden of Eden after Adam
and Eve are expelled (Genesis 3:24). Golden cherubim are at either
end of the mercy seat of the ark (Exodus 25:18-22) facing each other
with wings spread upward. In Ezekiel 10 the cherubim are the ones
that transport the glory throne of the Lord from the temple. Heber
pictures the cherubs and seraphs doing their worship work, and encourages us to join with them and fall down before the Lord. God,
who is the most worthy object of our worship, can be merely admired if we are not careful. Though some people enjoy singing about
God or even hearing talks about him, they will not cast down their
golden crowns before him as the elders did in the worship scene in
Revelation 4:2-11. They will not worship the saving, calling, gifting,
delivering God in three Persons.

In stanza three, Heber invites us to trust God even when we cannot
"see" his hand at work. This is difficult, isn't it? When the blessing of
Papa is evident for all to behold, testimonies to God's goodness flow
easily from our lips. The test of our mettle is what we sing and say
when the darkness hides him. Even when we cannot see his glory, it is
there, and so is God. When we are most tempted to doubt God's character, Heber reminds us he is perfect in power and love and purity.

While stanza four looks like a reprise of stanza one, it includes an
invitation for us to join all the created order in worship. Shame on us
if we allow the skies, rocks, trees and other inanimate objects to point
to God's power more than we do. Shame on us if birds out-sing us
and other animals display God's wonder more than we. Praise to God
should come from the earth (us), the sky and the sea.

This hymn, found in nearly every hymnal, is a potent reminder of
the great God we serve and the privilege we have to worship him.

Great Is Thy Faithfulness

A PORTRAIT OF
GOD'S TRUSTWORTHINESS

1. *Great is Thy faithfulness, O God my Father,*
   There is no shadow of turning with Thee;
   Thou changest not, Thy compassions, they fail not;
   As Thou hast been Thou forever wilt be.

Refrain:
   Great is Thy faithfulness!
   Great is Thy faithfulness!
   Morning by morning new mercies I see;
   All I have needed Thy hand hath provided—
   Great is Thy faithfulness, Lord, unto me!

2. *Summer and winter and springtime and harvest,*
   Sun, moon, and stars in their courses above
   Join with all nature in manifold witness
   To Thy great faithfulness, mercy, and love.

3. *Pardon for sin and a peace that endureth,*
   Thy own dear presence to cheer and to guide
   Strength for today and bright hope for tomorrow,
   Blessings all mine, with ten thousand beside!

THOMAS O. CHISHOLM, 1923

You've seen the ad in print or on television. A young couple inserts a test strip into a small urine sample. Seconds later they know whether or not they are going to have a baby. Though it is not a substitute for an exam by an obstetrician, the test allows folks to get an early warning that their lives are about to change. The ads promise that the tests are highly reliable. Several companies have taken this a step further. While reading and researching this chapter, I was made aware of an "Infidelity Test Kit." If you are suspicious that your spouse has been cheating on you, certain chemicals from the kit can be applied to the spouse's undergarments to detect traces of semen. How sad that the fidelity of some must be proven. For many, fidelity is a nearly impossible state to achieve.

The Bible contains no such kit for God, because he is ever faithful. His fidelity is one of the foundational doctrines of our faith. It is crucial to our understanding of who we are as God's people. If God cannot be counted on, our faith is shaky. Even our suffering can be understood as a manifestation of God's faithfulness. Robert Murray M'Cheyne, a nineteenth-century preacher (1813-1843), wrote a sermon on God's faithfulness.

> At the very time when Zion was saying, "My God hath forgotten me", God had her walls engraven on His hands, Isaiah 49:16. Look still to Jesus, oh! deserted soul. The love of God shines unchangeably on Him. Abide in Him and you will abide in the Father's love. Your afflictions may only prove that you are more immediately under the Father's hand. There is no time that the patient is such an object of tender interest to the surgeon, as when he is bleeding beneath his knife. So you may be sure if you are suffering from the hand of a reconciled God, that His

eye is all the more bent on you. "The eternal God is thy refuge, and underneath are the everlasting arms."[1]

Even when we're bleeding? When we sing of God's fidelity, we are reminding ourselves that in adverse circumstances we *also* see the hand of the Eternal. God is not only near to us and faithful to us in sunshine, he is also the personification of constancy in life's storms.

Had God been faithful to people who were also faithful to him, this hymn would not be notable. But the truth is God is loyal to scoundrels. He is faithful to people who have been spiritual adulterers. We have flirted with some gods and followed others. Yet our God remains *for* us. Faithfulness is part of God's character. It is not simply that he practices faithfulness; better than that, he *is* faithfulness.

"Know therefore that the LORD your God is God; he is the faithful God, keeping his covenant of love to a thousand generations of those who love him and keep his commands" (Deuteronomy 7:9). James 1:17 and the first stanza of this hymn remind us that God's signature trait is constancy. In him there is no variation or shifting shadow. Even if we are faithless, God will remain faithful (2 Timothy 2:13).

British preacher A. W. Pink (1886-1952) said, "God has not only told us the best, but He has not withheld the worst." Again Pink wrote, "He is faithful in what He withholds, no less than in what He gives."[2]

The second stanza of this hymn cites nature as an illustration of God's constancy. Summer, winter, spring and fall all make statements about God. The constancy of these seasons is a reflection of our God, in whom there is no variation. In the book of beginnings, God make a key statement to Noah, regarding God's commitment to humanity. "As long as the earth endures, seedtime and harvest, cold and heat, summer and winter, day and night will never cease" (Genesis 8:22). In Jeremiah's prophecy, God uses the unchanging rhythm of nature to reaffirm his commitment to Israel:

> This is what the LORD says,
> he who appoints the sun
>   to shine by day,
> who decrees the moon and stars
>   to shine by night,
> who stirs up the sea
>   so that its waves roar—
>   the LORD Almighty is his name:
> "Only if these decrees vanish from my sight,"
>   declares the LORD,
> "will the descendants of Israel ever cease
>   to be a nation before me."
>
> This is what the LORD says:
> "Only if the heavens above can be measured
>   and the foundations of the earth below be searched out
> will I reject all the descendants of Israel
>   because of all they have done,"
>   declares the LORD. (Jeremiah 31:35-37)

The unchanging nature of nature would have to change, and the heavens and earth would have to be measured before God would alter his love for his own. This realization makes me sing this hymn differently. God is *for* me. The constancy of the created order is a convincing demonstration of God's fidelity. However, there is more.

The third stanza of this hymn points to our personal salvation as another illustration. The natural order is external. "Pardon for sin and a peace that endureth" are internal realities. There are two primary positions in the Christian church regarding our salvation. Some believe that when we surrender our lives to Jesus the Christ, he forever keeps us and we are never snatched out of his hand. Others believe that salvation's hold on us is tenuous and that through acts of rebellion and disobedience, a believer may be lost even after saying "yes" to Christ. The writer of this hymn makes it clear that he believes that

pardon for sin and peace *endureth*. God's active presence in the lives
of his own is another illustration of his faithfulness. My father and
mother separated when I was eight years old. While I watched other
couples stay together I wondered why my parents didn't or couldn't.
Over against relationships that falter and fail stands a God who never
does. He commits himself not only to the earth but also to individu-
als. "Let us hold unswervingly to the hope we profess, for he who
promised is faithful" (Hebrews 10:23).

Christ is faithful as a son (Hebrews 3:6). He is faithful as a Savior
(John 10:27-29). He is faithful as a keeper (John 6:39). The reason
we are not worse off is because our God is faithful. Every morning,
says the refrain of this hymn, we see new expressions of God's mercy.

> *Because of the LORD's great love we are not consumed,*
>   *for his compassions never fail.*
> *They are new every morning;*
>   *great is your faithfulness. (Lamentations 3:22-23)*

Roger Simms, hitchhiking his way home, would never forget May 7.
His heavy suitcase wore him down. He was anxious to take off his army
uniform once and for all. Flashing the hitchhiking sign to the oncom-
ing car, he lost hope when he saw it was a black, sleek, new Cadillac.
To his surprise the car stopped, and the passenger door opened. He ran
toward the car, tossed his suitcase in the back and thanked the hand-
some, well-dressed man as he slid into the front seat.

"Going home for keeps?"

"Sure am," Simms responded.

"Well, you're in luck if you're going to Chicago."

"Not quite that far. Do you live in Chicago?"

"I have a business there. My name is Hanover." After talking about
many things, Simms, a Christian, felt a compulsion to witness to this
fiftyish, apparently successful businessman about Christ. But he kept
putting it off till he realized he was just thirty minutes from his home.

It was now or never. So Simms cleared his throat and said, "Mr. Hanover, I would like to talk to you about something very important." He then proceeded to explain the way of salvation, ultimately asking Mr. Hanover if he would like to receive Christ as his Savior. To Simms's astonishment the Cadillac pulled over to the side of the road. Simms thought he was going to be ejected from the car. But the businessman bowed his head and received Christ, then thanked Simms. "This is the greatest thing that has ever happened to me."

Five years went by. Simms married, had a two-year-old son and a business of his own. Packing his suitcase for a business trip to Chicago, he found the small white business card Hanover had given him five years before. In Chicago he looked up Hanover Enterprises. A receptionist told him it was impossible to see Mr. Hanover, but he could see Mrs. Hanover. A little confused as to what was going on, he was ushered into a lovely office and found himself facing a keen-eyed woman in her fifties. She extended her hand. "You knew my husband?" she asked.

Simms told how her husband had given him a ride when hitchhiking home after the war.

"Can you tell me when that was?"

"It was May 7, five years ago, the day I was discharged from the army.

"Anything special about that day?"

Simms hesitated. Should he mention witnessing to Mr. Hanover? Having come so far, he decided to take the plunge. "Mrs. Hanover, I explained the gospel to your husband. He pulled over to the side of the road and wept against the steering wheel. He gave his life to Christ that day."

Explosive sobs shook her body. Getting a grip on herself, she sobbed, "I had prayed for my husband's salvation for years. I believed God would save him."

"And," said Simms, "where is your husband, Mrs. Hanover?"

"He's dead," she wept, struggling with words. "He was in a car crash after he let you out of the car. He never got home. You see——I thought God had not kept His promise." Sobbing uncontrollably, she added, "I stopped living for God five years ago because I thought He had not kept His word!"[3]

There is no need to take a hiatus in your following of our God. As you sing this hymn, decide you will forever live for God, for he is ever and always committed to you.

SECTION 2

About Christ

8

O Come, O Come, Emmanuel

IMAGINING A
PRE-CHRISTIAN CONDITION

1. O come, O come, Emmanuel,
   And ransom captive Israel,
   That mourns in lonely exile here,
   Until the Son of God appear.

Refrain:
   Rejoice! Rejoice! Emmanuel
   Shall come to thee, O Israel.

2. O come, Thou Wisdom from on high,
   Who orders all things mightily;
   To us the path of knowledge show,
   And cause us in her ways to go.

3. O come, Thou Rod of Jesse, free
   Thine own from Satan's tyranny;
   From depths of hell Thy people save,
   And give them victory o'er the grave.

4. O come, Thou Day-spring, come and cheer
   Our spirits by Thine advent here;
   Disperse the gloomy clouds of night,
   And death's dark shadows put to flight.

5. O come, Thou Key of David, come
   And open wide our heavenly home;
   Make safe the way that leads on high,
   And close the path to misery.

6. *O come, O come, great Lord of might,*
   Who to Thy tribes on Sinai's height
   In ancient times once gave the law
   In cloud and majesty and awe.

7. *O come, Thou Root of Jesse's tree,*
   An ensign of Thy people be;
   Before Thee rulers silent fall;
   All peoples on Thy mercy call.

8. *O come, Desire of nations, bind*
   In one the hearts of all mankind;
   Bid Thou our sad divisions cease,
   And be Thyself our King of Peace.

LATIN HYMN, AUTHOR UNKNOWN
TRANSLATED 1851 BY JOHN M. NEALE

$\mathcal{T}$his hauntingly beautiful carol is based on one of the seven "O Antiphons," which were recited or chanted in the early church as worshipers celebrated the titles of the Messiah during the Advent season. More specifically, the "O Antiphons" were used during the period of preparation called the Octave before Christmas (December 17-23). Boethius (c. 480-524) makes a reference to the "O Antiphons" in his writing, so we know they have been part of the liturgy of the church for centuries. In addition to proclaiming a title of Christ, each antiphon contains a reference to Isaiah's prophecy of Christ.

- O Sapienta (O Wisdom, Isaiah 11:2-3; 28:29)
- O Adonai (O Lord, Isaiah 33:22)
- O Radix Jesse (O Root of Jesse, Isaiah 11:1, 10)
- O Clavis David (O Key of David, Isaiah 22:22; 9:7)
- O Oriens (O Rising Sun, Isaiah 9:2)
- O Rex Gentium (O King of the Nations, Isaiah 2:4)
- O Emmanuel (O God with us, Isaiah 7:14)

When I lead candlelight services during Advent, I remind worshipers that before Christ came, people walked in spiritual darkness (Isaiah 9:2). We imagine that darkness by turning out all the lights in the sanctuary. As we sit in the dark, I speak of the dreariness of sin and the despair of that life that has no light. We then light candles one at a time. As the room gradually gets lighter, I proclaim Christ, the Light of the world.

In this hymn, the worshipers ask Christ to come and rescue and ransom Israel. Most of us have never studied all the stanzas of this magnificent hymn of anticipation. Let's take a look.

The people called Israel had heard of this One who was to come.

They'd heard of him all their days and knew the story well. When the Messiah came he would right all wrongs, make the crooked places straight, the rough places plain and reveal God's glory. He would be the one to ransom captive Israel. A *ransom* is the price paid to secure the freedom of a person (Leviticus 19:20) or an animal (Leviticus 27:26-27). That economic metaphor became a grace-filled picture of what God did for Israel and for us. He paid the price that was on our heads so that we could be free. So the psalmist says,

> *He* ransoms *me unharmed*
> *from the battle waged against me,*
> *even though many oppose me.* (Psalm 55:18, emphasis mine)

Other passages clearly show our God as one who rescues us.

> *For the LORD will* ransom *Jacob*
> *and redeem them from the hand of those stronger than they.*
> (Jeremiah 31:11, emphasis mine)

> *I will* ransom *them from the power of the grave;*
> *I will redeem them from death.*
> *Where, O death, are your plagues?*
> *Where, O grave, is your destruction?*
> (Hosea 13:14, emphasis mine)

The New Testament teaches us that the paying of the ransom is the work of Jesus the Christ. "The Son of Man did not come to be served, but to serve, and to give his life as a *ransom* for many" (Matthew 20:28, emphasis mine).

In this hymn the writer has Israel acknowledging the need to be rescued. With that acknowledgment comes a direct appeal to the One capable of paying the full ransom. Note the rhythm of the hymn. Each stanza addresses Christ by a different name. The stanzas are prayerful requests. The refrain is an affirmation of the promise that the Rescuer-Deliverer *will* come. In stanza two the worshipers confess their need for wisdom. The source of that wisdom is the One who orders all things. Some of us grew up singing, in stanza two, "who orders all things far and nigh." Whether we sing that line or the one printed here, plainly we need help from the God of order. At Advent we bid farewell to chaos that we might welcome order. The third stanza addresses the promised Christ as the Rod of Jesse. "And there shall come forth a rod out of the stem of Jesse, and a Branch shall grow out of his roots" (Isaiah 11:1 KJV). The rescue motif continues as the descendant of Jesse is anticipated (Isaiah 11:10; Romans 15:12). He is the one who frees us from tyranny of all sorts. In addition to rescuing us, he cheers us. Don't miss this gift of the coming One. He scatters the gloom and doom and dark nights of the Israelites. Called "dayspring" (Luke 1:78 KJV), Christ, like the "rising sun" (NIV), brings brightness and hope.

So far, we are celebrating the coming Christ as rescuer, fount of wisdom, descendant of Jesse and the One who brings cheer. However, he comes not only to bring us something but also to take us somewhere—he is the Key of David (Isaiah 22:22; Revelation 3:7) who unlocks the heavenlies to us. Think of that paradise for which we are all morally and spiritually unqualified. We could not make it into that perfect place on our own. Even if we could, such a pathway would be filled with misery and danger. Benjamin Franklin said, "Those who would give up essential liberty to purchase a little temporary safety, deserve neither liberty nor safety."

This one whom Israel anticipates brings us liberty, makes the way safe and closes the path of misery. The safety he brings is not temporary but lasting. That reliable safety is rooted in the character of our God who, in Christ, never fails. A story is told of a monastery that was perched high on a three-thousand-foot cliff and accessible only by a terrifying ride in a swaying basket. Several strong men, perspiring under the strain of the fully loaded basket, pulled the basket with a single rope. A tourist who visited the site got nervous halfway up the cliff when he noticed that the rope was old and frayed. Hoping to relieve his fear, he asked, "How often do you change the rope?" The monk in charge replied, "Whenever it breaks!"

Hear the good news: God's rope never breaks. He takes his own to safety, and we can rely on him.

Again, it is easy for those of us in a post-Christian era to miss the import of this hymn. Imagine living in despair, then hearing the promise of the One who shall come, brightening our way and scattering our gloom. Lest we think he comes only to bring light, we are reminded in stanza six that he also brings law. Mount Sinai, on whose lofty peaks the law was given, is as much a part of the drama of redemption as is the picture of scattered darkness. This great Lord of might establishes his reign over Israel in the giving of the law. That display of power and rule is also a manifestation of worthiness. When one sees this mighty God for all he is, one can only respond in worship and awe. In my house, we only use the word *awesome* to refer to God and his mighty acts. We do not refer to pizza, cars and action scenes in movies as awesome. Awe is that wide-eyed, dropped-jaw response to the might of God. The witness of Israel to the watching nations was clearly tied to the awesome deeds of the law-giving God they followed. "If you do not carefully follow all the words of this law, which are written in this book, and do not revere this glorious and awesome name—the LORD your God—the LORD will send fearful plagues on you and your descendants, harsh and prolonged disasters, and severe and lingering illnesses" (Deuteronomy 28:58-59).

His self-revelatory display on Sinai as lawgiver set Yahweh apart from all other pretenders. In the third stanza, Christ is addressed as the Rod of Jesse, but in the seventh stanza, he is the Root of Jesse. What's the difference between the two titles? It is true that Christ is from the line of Jesse. Christ is the offspring of Jesse (Matthew 1:5-6). While he is the *fruit* of Jesse's line, he is also the *root* of it. He who was in the first century in Mary and Joseph's day was also in the beginning. As such, he is a sign for all people. This bold Sign of the People will cause rulers to fall in deference to him.

In Isaiah we see a word picture of Christ as the ensign of the people: "In that day the Root of Jesse will stand as a banner for the peoples" (Isaiah 11:10). He is not a banner whom all will choose to follow. However, whether one pledges allegiance to a flag or not, one cannot ignore the presence of the flag. The mighty and the small, the famous and infamous shall acknowledge the unfurled flag of our Christ.

The eighth stanza is a prayer we would do well to pray all year. Christ comes and brings peace where there has been discord. As Prince of Peace he alone binds nations and their peoples in one heart and mind. Only Christ can so transform us that we are no longer ruled by envy, strife and sorrow. Anyone who has heard a rendition of Handel's *Messiah* can hear in the inner ear, long after it's over, the bass soloist singing the words set in Haggai 2:6-7: "For thus saith the LORD of hosts; Yet once, it is a little while, and I will shake the heavens, and the earth, and the sea, and the dry land; And I will shake all nations, and the Desire of all nations shall come" (KJV).

Paul often pronounced peace upon those congregations to whom he wrote. His most common salutation was "Grace and peace to you from God our Father and from the Lord Jesus Christ" (Romans 1:7; 1 Corinthians 1:3; Ephesians 1:2). The One who is to come is both the source and bringer of peace.

Stephen Blank opens an article titled "Partners in Discord Only" this way:

> Despite presidential transitions in Russia and the United States, the bilateral relationship is and will remain troubled. Notwithstanding the end of the Cold War, the loud proclamation of a new "strategic partnership," and assertions, at least by American officials, of a significant community of interests between Washington and Moscow, growing rifts in interests, policies, status,

and perceptions are undermining relations beyond the point of mutual trust. While this discord has not precluded bilateral cooperation, even limited partnerships will prove difficult and remain the exception, not the rule, for the foreseeable future.[1]

The last line is arresting. For the foreseeable future we cannot expect peace among nations, because the Prince of Peace has been excluded from most discussions. So we continue to sing and pray, "O come, O come, Emmanuel, and rescue us."

9

And Can It Be?

OVERWHELMED
BY WONDER

1. And can it be that I should gain
   An interest in the Savior's blood?
   Died He for me, who caused His pain?
   For me, who Him to death pursued?
   Amazing love! how can it be
   That Thou, my God, shouldst die for me?

Refrain:
   Amazing love! how can it be
   That Thou, my God, shouldst die for me.

2. He left His Father's throne above,
   So free, so infinite His grace;
   Emptied Himself of all but love,
   And bled for Adam's helpless race;
   'Tis mercy all, immense and free;
   For, O my God, it found out me.

3. Long my imprisoned spirit lay
   Fast bound in sin and nature's night;
   Thine eye diffused a quick'ning ray;
   I woke, the dungeon flamed with light;
   My chains fell off, my heart was free;
   I rose, went forth, and followed Thee.

4. No condemnation now I dread;
   Jesus, and all in Him, is mine!
   Alive in Him, my living Head,
   And clothed in righteousness divine,
   Bold I approach th'eternal throne,
   And claim the crown through Christ my own.

CHARLES WESLEY, 1738

This great hymn starts out with wonder. Wesley is incredulous that he should have an interest, a part, in the Savior's blood. One can almost hear him asking, "Is it really true? Do I really have a part in the life and death of Jesus?" He continues his query, asking if Jesus died for the very one who caused his pain. Through to the end of stanza one, Wesley extols the amazing love of God and again asks how it can possibly be. One of the reasons I prefer to sing all stanzas of a hymn is because they frequently tell a story, which is ruined if we only sing a few stanzas. As this hymn progresses, Wesley tells the story of Christ's coming. Rarely has a more poignant celebration of Papa's saving power been set to music. In Philippians 2:5-7 we read:

> Your attitude should be the same as that of Christ Jesus:
> Who, being in very nature God,
> > did not consider equality with God something to be grasped,
> but made himself nothing,
> > taking the very nature of a servant,
> > being made in human likeness.

The single Greek word that is translated "made himself nothing" is a form of the verb *kĕnŏō*. Discussions and writings of this self-emptying of Christ are referred to, in theological studies, as the kenotic theory or kenosis of Christ. It means "to empty out, to make void" (Romans 4:14; 1 Corinthians 9:15), "to make of no effect" (1 Corinthians 1:17), "to be in vain" (2 Corinthians 9:3). With some poetic license, Wesley says that Jesus emptied himself of all but love and bled for us. I am sure Christ did not empty himself of everything except love. We know that from reading the Gospels, in which Jesus' many other attributes are seen. Jac J. Muller, in his commentary on Philippians, states it well: "At His incarnation He remained 'in the form of God' and as such He was Lord and Ruler over all, but He also accepted the nature of a servant as part of His humanity."[1] It is not that Christ uncluttered his life by laying aside his deity. It is that he humiliated himself, taking on the form and identity of sinful people, though he had not sinned. Wesley finds this amazing and staggering.

In the early church, believers regularly stood to affirm, in unison, what they believed about Jesus. In the fifth century, the Council of Chalcedon confessed: "Our Lord Jesus Christ, the same perfect in deity and the same perfect in humanity, truly God and the same truly man . . . one and the same Christ, Son, Lord, Only-Begotten, manifested in two natures, without confusion, without conversion, indivisibly, inseparably . . . the property of each preserved and combined into one person and one hypostasis." Christ had two sides that were not in confusion with each other—he was perfect God and perfect humanity. The Lutheran Augsburg Confession mentions, in Latin, "*Unus Christus, vere Deus, et vere homo*"—"one Christ, very [true] God and very [true] man." The Reformed Westminster Confession speaks of the incarnate Christ: "two whole, perfect, and distinct natures, the Godhead and the manhood, were inseparably joined together in one person . . . very God and very man, yet one Christ." Christ did not become something less than he was. He became something else, something in addition to who he already was.

Our glorious Lord did not suppress his divine attributes in his life and death. He took on humanity and took on our sin. Wesley, musing on the nature of Christ, finds it difficult to believe that he was so wonderfully transformed by Christ. The One who left his Father's throne was motivated by mercy. The poet William Blake (1757-1827) wrote

Where Mercy, Love, and Pity dwell
There God is dwelling too.

In *The Merchant of Venice*, William Shakespeare said, "The quality of mercy is not strained, It droppeth as the gentle rain from heaven Upon the place beneath: It is twice blest; It blesseth him that gives and him that takes." Wesley would certainly acknowledge that we are better off and blessed indeed, because of the mercy of Christ. That mercy was "immense and free"—this phrase is critical to our understanding of this hymn. W. E. Vine, in his *Expository Dictionary of New Testament Words*, says that mercy assumes need on the part of the one who receives it and adequate resources on the part of the one who gives it. Had Christ's mercy been limited in its scope, only portions of humanity would have access to him. Had that mercy not been free, only the wealthy could obtain salvation. Wesley rejoices that the One who died for the helpless daughters and sons of Adam is and was the Christ who *gives* rather than *sells* himself.

In stanza three, Wesley describes his pre-Christian life as a prison. When the light of Christ shone into his dungeon-like life, all was changed. Sometimes when I lead congregations in the singing of this hymn, I ask them to remain seated, with one wrist atop the other as if bound by a chain, as we begin singing the third stanza. We sing slowly and softly, with heads bowed, imitating the darkness and sadness of the dungeon. When we get to the line, "My chains fell off, my heart was free," I ask them to stand, break the imaginary shackles from their wrists and hold their hands up, as if surrendering to the Liberator. What a powerful reminder. When we came to Christ, we did not merely become nice people. We were set free.

Because we have been set free, says stanza four, we are no longer condemned. Here Wesley takes his cue from Romans 8:1-2: "Therefore, there is now no condemnation for those who are in Christ Jesus, because through Christ Jesus the law of the Spirit of life set me free from the law of sin and death." We who were guilty are now free from guilt. We who were spiritually impoverished now possess all things in Christ. We who were aimless now have a Living Head. We who were spiritually naked are now clothed in righteousness divine. We who were shy are now bold. We who were alienated from Christ now claim him as our own.

In fact, Jesus came as the visible expression of the judgment of God. His light judged humanity's darkness. His perfection was a judgment on our imperfection. His ordered life was an indictment on our chaos. His obedience to the Father was a commentary on our disobedience.

Some years ago, I got to know a well-known person. Many had heard this person on radio, seen him on videos and read his books. As I sat with him in his office, I realized that I was where many of his admirers would love to be. I was *with* him. It was a thrill to be close to someone whom I had admired from a distance. Could it be? Was I really in his office? Was I chatting with this celebrity? As Wesley considered the One who surpasses all mere mortals, he experienced a similar thrill. Could it be? "Died He for me who caused His pain? . . . How can it be that Thou, my God, shouldst die for me?" We cannot answer this question. We can simply celebrate that fact that we are the recipients of Papa's amazing love.

Amazing Grace

WHEN GOD
REACHES DOWN

1. Amazing grace! How sweet the sound
   That saved a wretch like me!
   I once was lost, but now am found,
   Was blind, but now I see.

2. 'Twas grace that my heart to fear,
   And grace my fears relieved;
   How precious did that grace appear
   The hour I first believed.

3. Through many dangers, toils and snares,
   I have already come;
   'Tis grace hath brought me safe thus far,
   And grace will lead me home.

4. When we've been there ten thousand years,
   Bright shining as the sun,
   We've no less days to sing God's praise
   Than when we first begun.

JOHN NEWTON, 1779
FOURTH STANZA WRITTEN BY JOHN REESE

Grace is one of those words that is thrown around so often and so carelessly that we hardly know its meaning. "Grace our party with your presence, won't you, dear?" "Jackie always did have such style and grace." "At supper we always say grace." "I usually pay my mortgage on the first of the month, but there's a grace period until the middle of the month." The average person understands *grace* as a synonym for kindness, courtesy, style or charm. The Bible, however, sings a different song. The Scriptures define *grace* as that attribute of God, which moves him to deal with humanity on the basis of our need rather than our merit. For instance, let's remember that moment when we realized our sinful state and recognized our need for forgiveness. We needed forgiveness but didn't deserve it. We also couldn't earn or manufacture it. We couldn't buy it or borrow it. We couldn't steal it or lease it. We couldn't find a reasonable facsimile thereof. God entered the picture and gave us, undeserving as we are, his forgiveness. He acted selflessly and required nothing from us in exchange. Augustine, the North African theologian whom Paul Enns calls "the greatest theologian between Paul and Luther,"[1] had a memorable twist on the concept of grace. Augustine said that because of the fall, humanity's only freedom was the freedom to sin.

That's a good angle from which to view our dilemma. It is true that we are agents of free will, but given our depravity, we are free to make only depraved choices. Some have suggested that grace is a New Testament concept only and that in the Old Testament we find a different portrait of God. I strongly disagree, for in the entirety of Scripture, we have a picture of a God who calls and reaches out to his alienated creation.

> *The LORD, the LORD, the compassionate and gracious God,*
> *slow to anger, abounding in love and faithfulness. (Exodus 34:6)*

> *Now the LORD was gracious to Sarah as he had said, and the*
> *LORD did for Sarah what he had promised. (Genesis 21:1)*

> *But now, for a brief moment, the LORD our God has been*
> *gracious in leaving us a remnant and giving us a firm place in*
> *his sanctuary, and so our God gives light to our eyes and a*
> *little relief in our bondage. Though we are slaves, our God has*
> *not deserted us in our bondage. He has shown us kindness in*
> *the sight of the kings of Persia. (Ezra 9:8-9)*

> *The LORD is gracious and compassionate,*
> * slow to anger and rich in love. (Psalm 145:8)*

The New Testament passages that speak of grace are better known, the best known probably being Ephesians 2:8-9: "For it is by grace you have been saved, through faith—and this not from yourselves, it is the gift of God—not by works, so that no one can boast."

To sing this well-known hymn without an understanding of the concept of grace is to waste one's breath. It is as empty as going through Christmas without knowing the Christ whose birth the season commemorates.

Grace, variously defined, is the reaching down of an almighty God to the needs of his undeserving creation. Some would so dilute the meaning of this concept that they would suggest that grace is that free-flow forgiveness of God that covers all behavior no matter how vile. In that case, grace is a disgrace. Grace is not a license to do whatever pleases us. Grace is an expression of God's eternal love toward creatures who have spurned such love, yet know they need it. Grace has more to do with God's commitment to us than it does with our attractiveness to him. We are not so graceful and elegant that God is bowled over by us. We are not so accomplished in theological and social graces that God simply must do something for us.

The sound of grace is amazing, precisely because the actions of God on our behalf are so undeserved. If we were morally upstanding and righteous, we should not be surprised when God extends favor to us. It would be appropriate and expected. However, the truth is that "while we were still sinners, Christ died for us" (Romans 5:8). Grace is not reciprocity. It is a God-initiated rescue. In the Greek language, the word for grace is *charis*. God is the original charismatic, exuding grace from his very essence. Grace presupposes that we have no other source but God.

Newton refers to life's changes in his hymn. What one of us has not experienced some "dangers, toils and snares"? Who of us has not faced fear? We are completely unable to rescue ourselves from the claws of such circumstances. God graciously enters and brings us to himself. Forgiving us of our offense and putting us in right standing with God as we stand behind and in Jesus the Christ, God calls us righteous. Lawrence O. Richards has summed up the doctrine of grace well:

> Grace is a dramatic statement about the human condition. Each person is helpless, trapped in sin and incapable of pleasing God or winning his favor. Grace is a proclamation. It is the triumphant announcement that God in Christ has acted and has come to the aid of all who trust him for their eternal salvation. Grace is a way of life. Relying totally on Jesus to work within us, we experience God's own unlimited power, vitalizing us and enabling us to live truly good lives.[2]

John Newton spent some of his early years involved in the despicable trafficking of slaves. He thought he was unworthy of God's love. We all are. Newton used the best adjective to describe the sound of such a display of divine kindness—amazing! Everything that Newton learned after that confrontation with God's grace was also grace-wrought. For instance, grace taught Newton's heart to fear. That same grace also relieved Newton's fear. It was that same grace that brought Newton to where he was when he penned this hymn and that same grace would lead him home to heaven. Finally that grace is what will transport us "there" as well, where we will sing through the countless years of eternity of that grace . . . again.

All Hail the Power of Jesus' Name

A GLOBAL CALL
TO WORSHIP

1. *All hail the power of Jesus' name!*
   Let angels prostrate fall;
   Bring forth the royal diadem,
   And crown Him Lord of all;
   Bring forth the royal diadem,
   And crown Him Lord of all!

2. *Ye chosen seed of Israel's race,*
   Ye ransomed from the fall,
   Hail Him who saves you by His grace,
   And crown Him Lord of all;
   Hail Him who saves you by His grace,
   And crown Him Lord of all!

3. *Let ev'ry kindred, ev'ry tribe,*
   On this terrestrial ball,
   To Him all majesty ascribe,
   And crown Him Lord of all;
   To Him all majesty ascribe,
   And crown Him Lord of all!

4. *O that with yonder sacred throng*
   We at His feet may fall!
   We'll join the everlasting song,
   And crown Him Lord of all;
   We'll join the everlasting song,
   And crown Him Lord of all!

EDWARD PERRONET, 1779-1780
STANZA FOUR BY JOHN RIPPON, 1787

Only in the last few years have I seen this hymn as a call to the universe. I formerly thought the first line was suggesting that we give all to completely hail or acclaim Jesus. I saw it as another version of a line such as that from "Revive Us Again," which says "all glory and praise to the Lamb that was slain." However, Perronet's hymn is not merely saying that all acclaim should go to Jesus. He is saying more than that—he is inviting every creature to hail, to reverence the name of Jesus. It is a call to the universal created order to bow before Jesus the King. In fact, this is a fine missions hymn, as seen most notably in stanza three. Every kindred and every tribe on this earth is to ascribe majesty to our Lord Christ. The power of Jesus' name is a given for the church. We take for granted the truth that the name of Jesus towers above all others. That very assumption is challenged in our culture, which prides itself on its tolerance and its refusal to place one deity above another. "Let's not be narrow," we hear. We are invited to accept the idea that every religion has something to offer and that "there are many roads to God." As politically correct as that sounds, it violates the exclusivity, which the Bible teaches without apology.

"He [Jesus] is 'the stone you builders rejected which has become the capstone.' Salvation is found in no one else, for there is no other name under heaven given to men by which we must be saved" (Acts 4:11-12). Treating the name of Jesus as unique was not the idea of a group of narrow-minded believers. It was God's recognition of his own Son. When we sing and speak the name of Jesus, we are not referring to the sequence of letters in his name. The name refers to the person and the character of Jesus.

For some, the name of Jesus has become a legalistic phrase that must be added to the closing line of every prayer. A parishioner once asked me if every prayer had to end with "this we ask in the name of

Jesus, amen." I told her we did not have to say that phrase each time. She was of the opinion that to add that phrase was to obey our Lord's instructions. It is true that our Lord said, "And I will do whatever you ask in my name. . . . You may ask me for anything in my name, and I will do it" (John 14:13, 14). But that does not teach that we must intone the phrase "in the name of Jesus" at the conclusion of every prayer in order to validate it.

In the period in which our Lord lived, the name referred not so much to the letters as to the full authority of the person. As we would use the phrase "in the name of mercy I beg you to let the prisoner go," so the name of Jesus refers to bringing the fullness of his character to bear, rather than a sequence of alphabetic units. So when Jesus says we ought to ask in his name, he is reminding us that we have no right to go to God the Father without being escorted. We go to God in Christ's name, that is, with Christ's approval. We rely fully on Christ's authority, his character and his person. Whether we utter the phrase or not, all Christian prayer is in the name of Jesus. We can only come to God the Father by and through the Son. Giving honor to that name is inevitable. One day countless millions will say, "Jesus is Lord." Some will have repeated it many times before. Others will have never before that day acknowledged Christ's reign. When Paul considered these truths in the kenotic passage in his letter to the church at Philippi, he said:

> *Therefore God exalted him [Jesus] to the highest place*
> *and gave him a name that is above every name,*
> *that at the name of Jesus every knee should bow,*
> *in heaven and on earth and under the earth,*
> *and every tongue confess that Jesus Christ is Lord,*
> *to the glory of God the Father. (Philippians 2:9-11)*

Commenting on Philippians 2:10, John MacArthur says:

Some assume that the new name is Jesus because verse 10 says "At the name of Jesus every knee should bow." But that wasn't a new name; it was bestowed at birth—"You shall call his name Jesus, for it is He who will save His people" (Matthew 1:21). Nor is the name Jesus above every name. There have been a lot of people named Jesus. The only name mentioned in Philippians 2:9-11 that is above every name is Lord. In verse 11 Paul says, "Every tongue should confess that Jesus Christ is Lord." That is the only name God gave Christ that is above every name. Whoever is Lord is in control.[1]

This hymn does not suggest that we may crown Jesus as King and Lord. Quite the contrary, it acknowledges the present reign of Jesus the King, Jesus the Lord and asks us to join with the prostrated angels as they affirm his sovereignty.

Sister Beatty was one of the more colorful saints at the Trinity Baptist Church in the Bronx, where I grew up. She was a demonstrative worshiper and would frequently "get happy"—a descriptive phrase used in my tradition for one who was overcome by emotion while praising God. Getting happy could take the form of fainting, dancing in the aisle, waving one's arms, raising one's hands, screaming, "Thank you, Jesus" or just groaning aloud. In the Pentecostal Church we called it "shouting." When Sister Beatty would get happy, she'd lean over in her pew as if stricken. On the way down, she'd say, "Oh, hallelujah. They can't crown him 'til I get there." I chuckle when I think of heaven holding up the crowning of Jesus until Sister Beatty gets there. From the dawning of creation Christ was Lord and King of all. In 1 Timothy, Christ is called "the King eternal, immortal, invisible, the only God" (1 Timothy 1:17). Christ is the King who always was, is and ever shall be. When he shall be crowned, in the presence of the prostrated angels, it shall be an affirmation rather than a coronation. "All Hail the Power of Jesus' Name" is an invitation to join in the celebration of the reign of the King eternal. Perronet suggests that it is a privilege rather than an obligation, although it is that too. This falling down before the King eternal is not something to which we must be dragged. It is a posture we assume with gladness.

Do you hear the sense of wonder in stanza four? Perronet suggests that when we shall have this privilege of being with that sacred throng over yonder, we will simply join in the singing. We will join in singing and worshiping at the feet of the King eternal.

Psalm 96 celebrates the enthronement of God:

> *Splendor and majesty are before him;*
> *strength and glory are in his sanctuary.*
> *Ascribe to the LORD, O families of the nations,*
> *ascribe to the LORD glory and strength.*
> *Ascribe to the LORD the glory due his name;*
> *bring an offering and come into his courts.*
> *Worship the LORD in the splendor of his holiness;*
> *tremble before him, all the earth.*
> *Say among the nations, "The LORD reigns." (Psalm 96:6-10)*

Psalm 97 begins with a similar statement of God's reign. Neither God nor Christ becomes Lord the moment we decide to follow him. God is, and ever shall be, the King of the earth. He has given that sovereignty to his Son also, inasmuch as Christ is the exact representation of God's being (Hebrews 1:3). I have heard neophyte disciples speak of how they have "made Jesus Lord." The truth is, Jesus always has been Lord. Whether or not we have hailed him as such is another story, but surely we do not "make him Lord." The power of his name, to which Perronet refers, is a power that is older than we are, and is a power that is not at all contingent upon our cooperation with him. The Lord is King whether we say so or not. He does not await our "amen" before he proclaims his sovereignty. All hail!

Fairest Lord Jesus

GOING BEYOND THE
BEAUTIFUL SCENERY

1. Fairest Lord Jesus,
   Ruler of all nature,
   O Thou of God and man the Son!
   Thee will I cherish,
   Thee will I honor,
   Thou, my soul's Glory, Joy and Crown!

2. Fair are the meadows,
   Fairer still the woodlands,
   Robed in the blooming garb of spring:
   Jesus is fairer, Jesus is purer,
   Who makes the woeful heart to sing.

3. Fair is the sunshine,
   Fairer still the moonlight,
   And all the twinkling starry host:
   Jesus shines brighter, Jesus shines purer,
   Than all the angels heaven can boast.

4. Beautiful Savior!
   Lord of the nations!
   Son of God and Son of Man!
   Glory and honor, praise, adoration,
   Now and forevermore be Thine!

STANZAS 1-3 ANONYMOUS, CIRCA 1677
STANZA FOUR WRITTEN BY JOSEPH A. SEISS

$\mathcal{I}$n 1988 I took a course to become a certified scuba diver. I was eager to see the wonders of God's creation beneath the surface of the ocean. Enjoying a short boat ride en route to a dive site, my instructor and I chatted about our careers. When he found out I was a preacher, he told me he was spiritual in his own way. He went on to say that when he introduced people to the ocean, he felt he was doing the work of God. I quickly told him that what he was doing was a good thing, that he was an environmentalist perhaps or even an ecologically sensitive person. However, introducing people to the ocean is not a spiritual activity. Diving does not equal intimacy with the Eternal.

Centuries before our Lord Christ was born, humans worshipped the sun. It was thought that inasmuch as the sun had power, it could bestow power on us. This led to either a solar religion, in which the sun became an object of worship, or an ideology in which the sun was prominent. Either way, it is a dangerous posture, for it exalts that which was created over the Creator. If one believed that the source of light was to be adored, one would not have to go far to assume that wisdom came from that same source, for wisdom is a form of enlightenment. Given that way of thinking, the sun may serve either as an object of worship or as a deity to be consulted. In nineteenth-century North America, there were a number of Native American tribes that observed the Sun Dance annually. It served as a reaffirmation of the practitioners' need for power. Eventually this dance became physically dangerous, as dancers would abstain from food or drink for several days at a time. Then they would fall in complete exhaustion. In 1904 the United States government banned the Sun Dance, fearing that many would die of exhaustion.

Before you pat yourself on the back and claim that you would never worship the sun, ask yourself a few questions: Have I ever given an inanimate object the reverence, the respect, the adoration that I ought to give to God? Have I become so enamored with an outdoor experience that I have literally become a sun worshiper? It's not that nature shouldn't be appreciated. In fact, our appreciation of the natural created order pleases the God who created it. What offends him is when something he has made takes the position that is rightly his. Do you remember the indictment against the Romans? They "exchanged the truth of God for a lie, and worshiped and served created things rather than the Creator—who is forever praised" (Romans 1:25).

I fly a small single-engine airplane to most of my preaching engagements. I am often asked what I do to pass the time as I am flying. One of my favorite activities in the air is to give thanks to Papa God for what I see. I immensely enjoy the beauty of creation. I watch clouds as they seem to float through the sky and waves as they appear to dance on the surface of ponds, streams, lakes and rivers. I have marveled at the astounding palette of nature's Painter as I've driven through New England in the fall. All these sights are from God, given for our enjoyment. However, the Christ whom God sent is even more beautiful than these.

What makes Jesus fairer? It is not his physical appearance. We have what some would consider a physical description of Jesus in the last book of the Bible: "And among the lampstands was someone 'like a son of man,' dressed in a robe reaching down to his feet and with a golden sash around his chest. His head and hair were white like wool, as white as snow, and his eyes were like blazing fire. His feet were like bronze glowing in a furnace, and his voice was like the sound of rushing waters. . . . His face was like the sun shining in all its brilliance" (Revelation 1:13-16). However, Isaiah said that Christ

> had no beauty or majesty to attract us to him,
>   nothing in his appearance that we should desire him.
> (Isaiah 53:2)

No, it is not his physical beauty that would make Jesus fairer. It is his character and his redemptive work that set him apart and make him shine "purer than all the angels heaven can boast." Jesus' character was flawless. What scars us and makes us ugly is our rebellion. Our disobedience robs us of our beauty. Jesus, in complete compliance with the Father's will, had no such blemishes. He lived in perfect union with the One who sent him. Therefore, he retains his standing with God, who sees the Son as beautiful. Even nature doesn't retain its beauty always. Trees rot and die. Oceans become murky and unpleasant places for swimming. Skies become hazy and smoggy. Green meadows turn brown. But Jesus shines brighter. While nature dims, Jesus becomes more radiant. Christ must ever be the Superlative. We are not forbidden in Scripture to appreciate the natural order. We are, however, forbidden to raise it above the eternal Christ, whom God sent for us.

While writing this chapter, I searched the Internet for any websites containing the words "worship+nature." The first site to come up was a New Age site that taught on its first page:

> Our goal is the creation of happy and natural individuals who are free to explore their own natures; individuals who are free to find new ways of being—and of relating to others—unfettered by convention or tradition.
>
> We could also say that it's about worshipping Nature, as long as you understand that we don't mean groveling before it as though it were some kind of static entity outside yourself, but rather reverence for it as a dynamic process of which you are a part.

Herein lays the great temptation of our culture. We are prone to ascribe to anything and anybody that reverence which belongs only and always to the living God who has revealed himself in Scripture and in nature and in Jesus the Christ. That which is created—the natural order, the elements of nature—must not be worshiped in place of the One who fashioned them.

In another hymn about the created order, Folliot S. Pierpoint observes nature but does not worship it. Instead, he uses such gazing to prompt him to worship.

For the Beauty of the Earth
For the beauty of the earth
For the glory of the skies,
For the love which from our birth
Over and around us lies.

Refrain:
Lord of all, to Thee we raise,
This our hymn of grateful praise.

For the beauty of each hour,
Of the day and of the night,
Hill and vale, and tree and flower,
Sun and moon, and stars of light.

Similarly, in the following Celtic prayer, nature causes us to look to the King of creation.

Rune of the "Muthairn"
Thou King of the moon
Thou King of the sun,
Thou King of the planets,
Thou King of the stars,
Thou King of the globe,
Thou King of the sky,
Oh! lovely Thy countenance,
Thou beauteous Beam.

As stunning as a sunset is, it ought only move us to give praise to the God who shines more brightly than that sun. Why stop at a reverence for the moon when you can know the God who flung it out into space? It is true, according to Psalm 19, that the heavens declare the glory of God. But declaration *by* the heavens is not permission to give worship *to* the heavens. We spend our days not in praise of creation but in glad acknowledgment that creation itself praises God (Psalm 19). When we behold hill and vale and tree and flower, it ought to be a call to worship the Creator, the living God.

Christ alone is preeminent. Worship him. He is fairer than the most arresting scene you've ever seen.

13

In the Garden

AN INVITATION TO AN
EMOTIONAL EXPERIENCE

1. I come to the garden alone,
   While the dew is still on the roses;
   And the voice I hear, falling on my ear;
   The Son of God discloses.

Refrain:
   And He walks with me,
   And He talks with me,
   And He tells me I am His own,
   And the joys we share as we tarry there,
   None other has ever known.

2. He speaks, and the sound of His voice
   Is so sweet the birds hush their singing,
   And the melody that He gave to me,
   Within my heart is ringing.

3. I'd stay in the garden with Him
   Though the night around me be falling,
   But He bids me go, through the voice of woe,
   His voice to me is calling.

C. AUSTIN MILES, 1912

The more we give ourselves to academic training and inquiry, the more uncomfortable this hymn becomes. After all, we who honor the life of the mind have been told that we need to minimize our reliance on experience as a valid measurement of truth. It does not matter how we feel; it's more important to know the facts. In some evangelistic literature I have seen a drawing of a railroad train as an illustration of the Christian life. The engine of the train was labeled "facts." The next car was called "faith," and the caboose was called "feeling." Most people who guided neophytes through the literature of this ministry group would tell them that the Christian experience is based on facts, which are responded to in faith. Feelings were an extra on the rear of the train. We could do without them, if we so desired. This is nonsense! We have been fashioned by a God who is himself full of emotion.

The Greeks used to teach that God, in order to be God, would have to be above or beyond feeling. If he had emotion, then we could sway him or even control him, emotionally. To protect their theology, the Greeks therefore taught that God was *apatheia*, literally without feeling. In a grand response to this concept, the writer of the epistle to the Hebrews said of Jesus: "For we do not have a high priest who is unable to sympathize with our weaknesses" (Hebrews 4:15). We do not have an apathetic God. This hymn dares to suggest we feel something as we reflect on the post-resurrection appearance of our Lord.

This hymn is based on the story found in John 20:11-18, which is both an objective and a subjective passage. It is objective in that it is a written record that does not change, giving us historical data regarding a conversation between Mary and Jesus the Christ. On the other hand, it is subjective as one is invited to have a similar experience and "walk" with the Risen One.

These days we are enjoying a spate of songs based solely on Scripture. I applaud this, since Christians should think deeply and honor God with our minds. In his book *Habits of the Mind* James Sire says, "All Christians are called to be as intellectual as befits their abilities and the work they have been called to do. No one is called to be a sloppy thinker."[1] Is there a place for a song that unashamedly encourages experience rather than facts? While we do not advocate a faith that forces us to choose between our hearts and our minds, let us also not encourage an experience with Jesus that presupposes we have no feelings. Bouncing off Sire, let me suggest that no one is called to be a sloppy feeler.

In the Gospel of Mark we read of our Lord and his compassion: "A man with leprosy came to him and begged him on his knees, 'If you are willing, you can make me clean.' Filled with compassion, Jesus reached out his hand and touched the man. 'I am willing,' he said. 'Be clean'" (Mark 1:40-41). Again we read: "When Jesus landed and saw a large crowd, he had compassion on them, because they were like sheep without a shepherd" (Mark 6:34). And "During those days another large crowd gathered. Since they had nothing to eat, Jesus called his disciples to him and said, 'I have compassion for these people; they have already been with me three days and have nothing to eat. If I send them home hungry, they will collapse on the way, because some of them have come a long distance'" (Mark 8:1-3).

Did you see it? The Lord of Glory has a heart. He is not some cold, unfeeling deity. He is the Son of God and the Son of humanity. He doesn't look at a crowd without being moved.

Few hymns have as emotional a story attached to them as does "In the Garden." In fact, many readers will find the composer's account of how he came to write this hymn a bit too experiential.

One day in March 1912, I was seated in the dark room, where
I kept my photographic equipment and organ. I drew my Bible

toward me; it opened at my favorite chapter, John 20—whether by chance or inspiration let each reader decide. That meeting of Jesus and Mary had lost none of its power to charm. As I read that day, I seemed to be part of the scene. I became a silent witness to that dramatic moment in Mary's life, when she knelt before her Lord, and cried, "Rabboni!" My hands were resting on the Bible while I stared at the light blue wall. As the light faded, I seemed to be standing at the entrance of a garden, looking down a gently winding path, shaded by olive branches. A woman in white, with head bowed, hand clasping her throat, as if to choke back her sobs, walked slowly into the shadows. It was Mary. As she came to the tomb, upon which she placed her hand, she bent over to look in, and hurried away. John, in flowing robe, appeared, looking at the tomb; then came Peter, who entered the tomb, followed slowly by John.

As they departed, Mary reappeared, leaning her head upon her arm at the tomb, she wept. Turning herself, she saw Jesus standing, so did I. I knew it was He. She knelt before Him, with arms outstretched and looking into His face cried "Rabboni!"

I awakened in full light, gripping the Bible, with muscle tense and nerves vibrating. Under the inspiration of this vision I wrote as quickly as the words could be formed the poem exactly as it has since appeared. That same evening I wrote the music.[2]

I know this might sound too mystical for some readers, but we cannot deny another's experience. A musician complained to a friend of mine that many hymns were musically and textually "bad." My friend replied, "Hymns are people's stories and there are no bad stories." We don't have to understand or accept another's story, but we surely cannot say it did not happen.

In the faith tradition of which I am a part, experience is very important. In addition to academic preparation for ministry, it is expected that those of us who minister will also have a fire within. It is expected that we have been in the garden with Jesus. When I was a teen I was the pianist for a small congregation in the Bronx. After I'd play the piano at my home church during the early worship celebration, I'd board a bus and go to that little church. The pastor of that congregation said to me, "Richard, one day you're going to preach. Don't you ever let me catch you preaching about Daniel in the lion's den . . . 'til you been in one!" Faith is to become so personalized that it might be said of us, "They have been with Jesus." Mary found it to be so in John 20, as did C. Austin Miles, as did I.

The good news is that you also may experience Jesus. We never need to apologize that we feel Jesus, that we have known him in a nonacademic way. This presupposes that we stay in the garden with him, though the night around us be falling. In fact, I submit that the ability to bear witness to Jesus in the world is a direct result of our having been with him in the garden. It is the experience of having walked and talked with Jesus in the garden and hearing his affirming "you are my own" that empowers us to represent him outside the garden.

In the Cross of Christ I Glory

A SYMBOL THAT
CHANGES US

1. In the cross of Christ I glory,
   Towering o'er the wrecks of time;
   All the light of sacred story
   Gathers round its head sublime.

2. When the woes of life o'ertake me,
   Hopes deceive, and fears annoy,
   Never shall the cross forsake me,
   Lo! it glows with peace and joy.

3. When the sun of bliss is beaming
   Light and love upon my way,
   From the cross the radiance streaming
   Adds more luster to the day.

4. Bane and blessing, pain and pleasure,
   By the cross are sanctified;
   Peace is there that knows no measure,
   Joys that through all time abide.

JOHN BOWRING, 1825

$\mathcal{M}$any of the stories connected with this hymn are apocryphal at best and outright fallacies at worst. Though we cannot historically substantiate the story connected with the writing of this text, it is a plausible one. It is said that John Bowring was once sailing along the coast of China and saw an abandoned church building with a massive cross atop it. This scene was the inspiration for this fine hymn. We see the cross of Christ towering over all things, periods of time, people and events.

It seems that a scene as gory as the cross would compel one to run *from* the scene. Yet we as believers run *to* the cross. We embrace it. We "cling to the old rugged cross."

Every religious tradition has its symbols that evoke entire histories, theological constructs, cultural stances and doctrinal positions. Christians have the fish. Early followers of Christ used a fish to identify each other in prisons and in the marketplace. The Greek word for fish, *ichthus,* is spelled *Iota Chi Theta Upsilon Sigma*, which is an acrostic for Jesus Christ, of God, the Son, the Savior—*Iesous*: Jesus, **Chr**istos: Christ, **Theou**: of God, **Uiou**: the Son, **Soter**: the Savior.

I	Iesous (Jesus)
X	Christos (Christ)
Θ	Theos (God's)
Y	Uios (Son)
Σ	Soter (Savior)

Jews have the menorah, which is a candelabrum with seven or nine candles, used to commemorate the light of Yahweh following Israel on their journey. It is still used in synagogues and homes in the observance of Hanukkah. Jews also have the Star of David consisting of two interlocking triangles. The resulting six-point star is seen on the Israeli flag and in every synagogue. It was said that King David's soldiers had a symbol emblazoned on their shield. In Hebrew, it is called *Magen David,* literally, the shield of David.

Buddhists use lotus blossoms, which for centuries have served as a symbol of enlightenment. The lotus symbolizes purity, peace and compassion, loveliness and fertility. Legend has it that when the infant Lord Buddha took his first seven steps, a lotus blossom grew from each of his footprints. This flower is sacred to both Hindus and Buddhists.

Muslims have the crescent moon. Many sources suggest that the crescent moon was originally a symbol of the Ottoman Empire, which ruled over Turkey for some time. Whether the symbol originated with Islam or not, it is by now a globally recognized symbol of the Muslim belief system.

Ancient Egypt used the scarab beetle as its religious symbol. Legend has it that the beetle rolled a dung ball around, which eventually became the sun and the beetle rolled the sun across the sky. Doing this daily, the beetle saw to it that the Egyptians had sun.

In this hymn, Bowring suggests that Christians actually glory in the cross. We followers of Christ celebrate the cross—not that we extol that instrument of torture; rather, we rejoice in what happened there. For us the cross is the preeminent symbol of a great drama. We are not making the wooden object an icon. For us, the importance is not the object, but the objective—what Christ came to earth to accomplish culminated in the cross event. The Greek word for cross, *stauros*, means "post" or "stake." When our Lord Christ was nailed to the stake, all our waywardness, rebellion, disobedience and selfishness were nailed there also.

In stanza two, Bowring suggests that the event at the cross has power. Even when hopes are dashed and the fear factor high, the cross shall preserve us. Here Bowring calls for appropriate recall. When we remember what Christ experienced on our behalf, the woes and fears are put into perspective. "Never shall the cross forsake me." What confidence is this that allows one who is afraid and broken to make strong statements about the Christ of the cross? Once I have fully embraced the event of the cross, the power thereof is mine. I refer to that event as a life-defining moment. People of the cross don't simply think of agony when they see a representation of the cross. Agony, however, is part of the drama. We don't merely think of humiliation although it is there. We think of the saving, sustaining power of the living God. The cross, more specifically, the memory of what happened there, shall keep us. In what seems an inappropriate reference to the cross, Bowring says that "it glows with peace and joy." The kitsch of some religious bookstores aside, when was the last time you saw a glowing cross? Not often do we connect torture to joy. Yet Bowring writes that a life in the cross can have, towering over it, the joy and peace of the crucified Christ.

When Paul penned his letters to the first-century followers of Christ, he used the cross as a synonym for the very message that he preached. It is not so much that he only preached on or about the death of Christ; rather, the drama of the cross was and is central to all that Paul proclaimed. So when he wrote to the Corinthians he said, "For Christ did not send me to baptize, but to preach the gospel—not with words of human wisdom, lest the cross of Christ be emptied of its power. For the message of the cross is foolishness to those who are perishing, but to us who are being saved it is the power of God" (1 Corinthians 1:17-18).

Having grown up in a multicultural housing project, I was exposed to religious traditions other than my own. I have clear memories of my Roman Catholic friends being confirmed and receiving their first communion. I clearly remember the gifts that the girls were given—necklaces with a crucifix or a simple cross in the center. I often wish another symbol of the Christian faith had been embraced. There are so many options. Why not a depiction of an empty tomb? A manger, a carpenter's hammer, a lamb, a star or a rose would have also been appropriate symbols for us. Yet we have the cross. Think not that reflecting on the cross is only for life's toughest circumstances. Even if you're having a great day, says Bowring, the cross adds more luster to it. It would be the height of misunderstanding if we were to keep the cross handy only for those days when we're feeling low. The cross never forsakes us, and we must never forsake it.

To say we are Christians is to also say we receive and embrace what happened at the cross. Classic Christian faith proclaims that we were never spiritually fit enough to stand before God. Being perfect, however, Christ was qualified to stand the scrutiny of a demanding, holy God. Christ became like us (through being born as a human) so that we might become like him. Christ took on our state so that we could take on his. Second Corinthians 5:21 says it well: "God made him [Christ] who had no sin to be sin for us, so that in him [Christ] we might become the righteousness of God." That truth is not to be pondered on alternate days of the week or in times of stress only. This magnificent love of God is ours to hold even "when the sun of bliss is beaming."

Sloppy theology would have us cooing over the baby in the manger but neglecting the drama of Calvary. It would have us sing carols about "Joy to the World" but have us avoid "O Sacred Head, Now Wounded." In a book written more than a century ago, James Denny wrote, "The New Testament knows nothing of an incarnation which can be defined apart from its relation to atonement. . . . Not Bethlehem, but Calvary, is the focus of revelation, and any construction of Christianity which ignores or denies this distorts Christianity by putting it out of focus."[1] Even though we know the story of God's love did not end with the event on the cross, that event is still central for us. Without the agony of Good Friday there would be no victory of the resurrection morn.

In the closing stanza, Bowring posits the most radical line of his hymn. He says that the good and the bad, the sunshine and the rain, the blessing and the bane (Old English word meaning "poison, ruin and woe") are all sanctified by the cross.

When I was a youngster, my next-door neighbor's grandmother became my surrogate grandmother. Although my two grandmothers lived in New York City as did I, and I saw them regularly, I enjoyed my surrogate grandmother. When she visited her own natural grandchildren, I enjoyed the visit as much. She was a Pentecostal evangelist, and I enjoyed going to the spirited worship services of the church she attended. In fact my traditional Baptist home church folks would have called that other church a "sanctified church." (That was and is the label given to the Pentecostals.) How tragic that we think a denomination or a tradition owns a biblical doctrine. To be sanctified is to be reserved for specific purposes. Our bodies are sanctified in that we use them only in the service of our God. Our talents and gifts are sanctified inasmuch as we use them for Yahweh's glory and not our own.

Bowring suggests that bane and blessing are reserved for the usefulness of God *by the cross*. Bowring does not promise life without pain or bane. Rather, Bowring offers the possibility of our having our perspective changed. Our circumstances are given a new look when they are passed through the sanctifying filter of the cross. If we had thoughts of wallowing in our pain or blaming God for the difficult times, Bowring suggests that we can hold our troubles up to the light of grace. Like a fine diamond, those problems are rotated in the light and we see shafts of light bouncing from each side and every angle. When we examine those troubles again, they are sanctified. In our processing of the bane and blessing, we get God's perspective. Isn't that what we want? Don't we want the mind of Christ? Don't we want to see life as he sees it? When Papa God is at work in the earth, he changes his people more often than he changes circumstances. Troubles do not disappear. More often, they are simply sanctified.

When we leave our pain and bane in the hands of our Papa God, we experience that often-elusive reality called peace. It is a gift of Jesus. "Peace I leave with you; my peace I give you. I do not give to you as the world gives" (John 14:27). Rather than our becoming anxious and fearful, we receive the peace of Jesus. This is not a feeling, but a taking to ourselves the confidence that is available because we are the people of Christ. Because he is alive and full of power, we need not fear. In fact, we may be bold in the face of pain and trouble. Why? Because the Prince of Peace is at work in our circumstances. Peace is more than the absence of conflict. The Hebrew word for "peace" is *shalom*. The word always refers to wholeness, unity, harmony and soundness. It is a confidence in the midst of the trials, which expresses confidence in One greater than the trouble.

Recently I took my pastor flying. He had just finished speaking at a retreat that day and was weary. While we were flying, he fell asleep. When he awakened, I told him I was pleased that he felt comfortable enough to take a nap while I flew the plane. When Jesus is at the controls of life, one need not fret. One can sleep, knowing that "peace is there that knows no measure." Glorying in the cross is not something we do only when times are tough. We glory in the cross as a way of life. The rugged cross is our reference point. In his engaging, thought-provoking, scholarly treatment on the subject of the cross, John R. W. Stott writes:

> For the peace which God secures is never cheap peace, but always costly. He is indeed the world's pre-eminent peacemaker, but when he determined on reconciliation with us, his "enemies," who had rebelled against him, he "made peace" through the blood of Christ's cross (Colossians 1:20). To reconcile himself to us, and us to himself, and Jews, Gentiles and other hostile groups to each other, cost him nothing less that the painful shame of the cross.[2]

Christ the Lord Is Risen Today

THE SONG OF THE EMPTY TOMB

1. *Christ the Lord is risen today, Alleluia!*
   Sons of men and angels say, Alleluia!
   Raise your joys and triumphs high, Alleluia!
   Sing, ye heavens, and earth, reply, Alleluia!

2. *Love's redeeming work is done, Alleluia!*
   Fought the fight, the battle won, Alleluia!
   Lo! the Sun's eclipse is over, Alleluia!
   Lo! He sets in blood no more, Alleluia!

3. *Vain the stone, the watch, the seal, Alleluia!*
   Christ hath burst the gates of hell, Alleluia!
   Death in vain forbids His rise, Alleluia!
   Christ hath opened paradise, Alleluia!

4. *Lives again our glorious King, Alleluia!*
   Where, O death, is now thy sting? Alleluia!
   Once He died our souls to save, Alleluia!
   Where thy victory, O grave? Alleluia!

5. *Soar we now where Christ hath led, Alleluia!*
   Following our exalted Head, Alleluia!
   Made like Him, like Him we rise, Alleluia!
   Ours the cross, the grave, the skies, Alleluia!

6. *Hail, the Lord of earth and heaven, Alleluia!*
   Praise to Thee by both be given, Alleluia!
   Thee we greet triumphant now, Alleluia!
   Hail, the resurrection day, Alleluia!

7. *King of glory, Soul of bliss, Alleluia!*
   Everlasting life is this, Alleluia!
   Thee to know, Thy power to prove, Alleluia!
   Thus to sing and thus to love, Alleluia!

8. *Hymns of praise then let us sing, Alleluia!*
   Unto Christ, our heavenly King, Alleluia!
   Who endured the cross and grave, Alleluia!
   Sinners to redeem and save. Alleluia!

9. *But the pains that He endured, Alleluia!*
   Our salvation have procured, Alleluia!
   Now above the sky He's King, Alleluia!
   Where the angels ever sing. Alleluia!

10. *Jesus Christ is risen today, Alleluia!*
    Our triumphant holy day, Alleluia!
    Who did once upon the cross, Alleluia!
    Suffer to redeem our loss. Alleluia!

CHARLES WESLEY, 1739

A young pastor assumed leadership of a very traditional parish and thought he'd try a new approach to Easter Sunday. He changed the music and the order of the worship service. Most of the parishioners found this disconcerting. As the ushers came forward to pray and then receive the morning offering, one of them had, on the plate, a note, which only the pastor could read. It said, "We are not leaving here this morning, and neither are you, until we sing 'Christ the Lord Is Risen Today.'" This hymn is one of the most popular hymns sung on Resurrection Day. I have memories of robed choirs, pastors and priests in full vestments and congregants in vibrant spring colors, singing "Alleluia!" There is not one sad word in this hymn. It is upbeat in its text and made regal in its alignment with the hymn tune Easter Hymn.

The first stanza dares us to raise high our joys and triumphs. The heavens and earth are to join in antiphonal singing. The heavens sing and the earth replies, "Alleluia!" In stanza two he reminds us that the work Christ came to do—delivering humanity from its vulnerability to sin's eternal consequences—was finished. The battle for the souls of humans was fought and won. The darkness that covered the land when Christ died was gone (Matthew 27:45). The bloody setting in which Christ was seen on Good Friday was no more.

In the third stanza, Wesley comments on those people and systems put in place to stop the forward march of Christ. The workers who prepared the stone with which Christ's tomb was sealed, as well as those who watched the tomb, worked in vain. Death itself, if it tried to prevent Christ's rising, acted in vain. In the Gospel of John, Jesus reminds us that he has prepared a place for us, so that where he is we may be also (John 14:2-3). In Wesley's hymn, paradise is that place.

On Resurrection Day we celebrate the fact that Christ who once was dead is now alive. Stanza four reminds us that this risen Christ has taken the sting out of death and robbed the grave of any alleged victory. That event, which occurred once and has eternal consequences, makes the grave a place devoid of victory. I wish you could have heard the preachers of my tradition years ago. They are not all gone, but there are fewer of them around now. It didn't matter where they began a sermon, they could very often end up preaching about the resurrection. They would describe the death of Christ. Then they would pause and say, "But early . . . early . . . early Sunday morning he got up with all power in his hands. Death tried to hold him. The grave tried to keep him. Satan tried to stop him. But he conquered death, hell and the grave." Then the old preachers would intone the words, "O death, where is thy sting? O grave, where is thy victory?" (1 Corinthians 15:55 KJV).

The hymn's fifth stanza says that as Christ soars into that place, so we, too, soar. As he is lifted, so we are lifted. What he endured and received, we endure and receive. Wesley says we are made like Christ, and like Christ, we rise. One is reminded of Paul's telling the Corinthians that "just as we have borne the likeness of the earthly man, so shall we bear the likeness of the man from heaven" (1 Corinthians 15:49). To be made like him is to be invited to the cross, the grave and the skies. Many of our hymnals have only four stanzas of this Wesleyan hymn. Those four stanzas are usually a patchwork of the original, with a few lines borrowed from stanzas five to ten. I have included all ten here so we could see what we have been missing. When all is sung and said, we find ourselves rejoicing that we know this Risen Conqueror.

Stanza seven says it well. Everlasting life is this: to know the King of Glory, the Soul of Bliss. We prove his power; we sing and we show his love.

A compound word, the word *alleluia* comes from the Hebrew verb *hallel*, "to praise," and from *Yah*, a shortened form of the name "Yahweh." To say and sing *alleluia* is to praise Yahweh, our great God. "Alleluia" is not only a recurring refrain in this hymn but ought to be the recurring chorus in a well-lived life. We say it when death seems victorious over life. We sing and say it in our pain. We shout it, oratorio-like, as if the whole world is listening to us sing Handel's "Hallelujah Chorus." A chorus sung in many churches says:

Hallelujah anyhow
Never let your troubles get you down
When life's troubles come your way,
Hold your head up high and say,
Hallelujah anyhow!

One gets the impression that Wesley was an "Alleluia anyhow" person. The victorious Christ was informing Wesley's life. The hymn's eighth stanza contains the perfect invitation: "Hymns of praise then let us sing. Alleluia!" Christ has endured the cross, procured our salvation and redeemed our loss. We who once feared death, the last enemy (1 Corinthians 15:26), need fear it no longer. Why not? Because Christ is the King of the skies. Alleluia!

O Love That Wilt Not Let Me Go

LOCKED UP AND FREE

1. O Love that wilt not let me go,
   I rest my weary soul in Thee;
   I give Thee back the life I owe,
   That in Thine ocean depths its flow
   May richer, fuller be.

2. O Light that followest all my way,
   I yield my flickering torch to Thee;
   My heart restores its borrowed ray,
   That in Thy sunshine's blaze its day
   May brighter, fairer be.

3. O Joy that seekest me through pain,
   I cannot close my heart to Thee;
   I trace the rainbow through the rain,
   And feel the promise is not vain
   That morn shall tearless be.

4. O Cross that liftest up my head,
   I dare not ask to fly from Thee;
   I lay in dust life's glory dead,
   And from the ground there blossoms red
   Life that shall endless be.

GEORGE MATHESON, 1882

$\mathcal{T}$his is, in my opinion, one of the most profound texts in our hymnals. Few texts are more thought provoking and image-laden. In each stanza the great Scottish preacher George Matheson calls God by one of his attributes. In stanza one God is love. In stanza two he is light. In stanza three he is joy, and in stanza four he is the cross. Rather than simply speaking of love, light, joy and suffering as concepts, Matheson personalizes them. When one considers the love of God, it is indeed a capturing love that refuses to let us go. In another of his hymns Matheson prays, "Make me a captive, Lord, and then I shall be free." It is a notable paradox that we are only free when we have been captured by God's love.

In June 1979 I was at the Hampton Ministers' Conference hosted by Hampton University. The late Dr. D. E. King was in attendance, and the moderator of the evening service asked him to come to the platform to pray. Dr. King was eloquent in preaching and praying. When he began his prayer I thought, *This is going to be good.* So I took out my notebook that is always with me and copied his prayer word for word. This is what Dr. King prayed: "We have come to turn ourselves in. We have been running from Thee and we know you have a warrant out for our arrest. Arrest us; lock us up, that we may be free."

George Matheson would undoubtedly agree that we are ultimately free when we have been made captives of the love of God. If God were only love, that would be exciting enough, but Matheson reminds us that God is also light. Three times in the New Testament we have direct definitions of God: God is spirit (John 4:24), God is love (1 John 4:16), and God is light (1 John 1:5). Matheson, totally blind by age eighteen, must have rejoiced in this. God dispels darkness. If God doesn't eradicate our physical blindness, he certainly does heal us of that blindness which is spiritual. When compared to the radiance of our God, all we have is a flickering torch and a borrowed ray. One may choose to either know the bright blaze of light personified or remain in the shadows of an all too fading, dimming light of one's own. In a very descriptive passage about the benefits of the Lord's coming, Isaiah says to Israel:

> *Arise, shine, for your light has come,*
> *and the glory of the LORD rises upon you.*
> *See, darkness covers the earth*
> *and thick darkness is over the peoples,*
> *but the LORD arises upon you*
> *and his glory appears over you.*
> *Nations will come to your light,*
> *and kings to the brightness of your dawn. (Isaiah 60:1-3)*

Let us celebrate with Matheson that God not only breaks light upon us, he also draws others to our lights. Let us also rejoice that our God *is* light. He wears it as a garment. Wherever God is there is at least the possibility of darkness being scattered.

If we had God as love and light only, that would be cause for exuberant celebration. But Matheson gives us more in this hymn.

God is seen as the joy that seeks and finds us in our pain. In the African American worship tradition there is a dialogue between the preacher and congregation, which rehearses the presence of God in our pain.

Pastor: Have you tried Jesus?
Congregation: Yes!
Preacher: Ain't he alright?
Congregation: Hallelujah.
Preacher: Have you tried him as a doctor?
Congregation: Yes, sir.
Preacher: Ain't he alright? Has he made a way out of no way?
Congregation: Glory!

Matheson reminds us that God is alright, that he seeks us in and through our pain; that God's promises about that great morning are not in vain. In clear terms, Matheson says we may trust this God to bring us joy and to be our joy. When he was six years old, my son was in the back seat as I drove him to school early one morning. I said, "Honey, are you going to have a great day today?"

"How should I know, Daddy?" he said.

I told him that we could control much of what went on that day. I told him that he could *decide* he was going to have a great day. Matheson says God is the joy that seeks us and gives us a good day. When God is our focus, the day is different. We see not only the rain but also the rainbow. Are you going to have a great day today?

In his final stanza, Matheson reads our minds, for many of us would like to avoid the cross. We don't mind seeking rainbows, but in doing so we'd like to avoid Calvary. Matheson will say that it is the Christ of the cross who lifts us. While we would ask to fly from the cross, Matheson dares us to behold it. The hardened ground of the cross becomes the fountain from which endless life can flow. This text invites us into union with the One who is variously described as love, light, joy, cross and more.

I was once asked if we had to use the salutation "Dear God" when we pray. I was happy to report to the inquirer that I'd read the Scriptures and discovered that God has numerous names. We could say "Dear Rock," and he will hear us. We could say, "Good morning, Light of the world," and he would answer. Matheson might pray, "Dear Love, Light, Joy and Cross." I am sure God would answer.

About the Church

Blest Be the Tie That Binds

CELEBRATING THE
FAMILY OF GOD

1. Blest be the tie that binds
   Our hearts in Christian love;
   The fellowship of kindred minds
   Is like to that above.

2. Before our Father's throne
   We pour our ardent prayers;
   Our fears, our hopes, our aims are one,
   Our comforts and our cares.

3. We share our mutual woes,
   Our mutual burdens bear;
   And often for each other flows
   The sympathizing tear.

4. When we asunder part,
   It brings us inward pain;
   But we shall still be joined in heart,
   And hope to meet to again.

JOHN FAWCETT, 1782

At the time of writing this book, I am in my early fifties and am celebrating the fact that I have been a part of the church by virtue of personal union with Christ for forty years. Even with a sizeable vocabulary at my disposal, I cannot adequately describe here all that the church means to me. When I was a youngster, we lived eight long city blocks from the Trinity Baptist Church. For many of those years the only way for us to get to the church building was to walk. In the winter that was not fun. But I made the trek gladly, for I loved going to worship. The Jackson family, with their ten children and two parents, lived in the same apartment building as our family. We would often look like a small mob as we all walked to church. Going to corporate worship was the highlight of my week. It still is.

The church is that body of people who have heard God calling them from something and to something. The Greek word for church, *ekklesia*, is a word made up of *ek* ("out of") and *kaleo* ("to call"). Literally, the church is an assembly of "called out" people. The same word is used for a gathering of citizens, whether lawful (Acts 19:39) or confused and unruly (Acts 19:32, 40-41). We get to the point where we need what a gathering of "called out" people has to offer. It calls us from self-centeredness to union with Christ. It calls us from avarice and materialism to service and sacrifice. In fact, what the church does is bind us. Which of us wishes to be bound? Certainly not I. I want my freedom. It's my right, my privilege. Rules and strictures are for children and prisoners, and I am not a part of either category. Actually, as freeing as those last three sentences sound, none of us would fare well in a system in which there are no limits. Imagine driving on a road with no speed limit in force. Think of a school year with no limit to the number of class days, exams or term paper requirements. Think of an adjustable rate mortgage with no limit to the amount of interest that you'd be charged.

All of us acknowledge the need for some limits. In the church our hearts are bound by a tie of Christian love. If one is to be bound, this is a desirable restraint. Over a period of months and years, as we interact with members of the congregation, we find ourselves bound together. In a day in which independence and individualism have such high values attached to them, this is a reality worth celebrating. There is a fellowship of kindred minds that begins to form (stanza one). Even people who are not lovers of Jesus need a gathering, an assembly. It is what makes some sports fans fight traffic and travel to a stadium rather than watch an event on television. There is a mystical something that we experience when we are together that we do not when we are apart. Witness the tailgate parties at a sports stadium. Hours before the game, some will park their vehicles, take out a barbecue grill, an ice chest of drinks and have a party.

TheMan.com is a start-up Internet company designed to advise men on everything from dating to choosing clothing. The September 27, 1999, issue of *Time* magazine described a start-up company's corporate culture. The articles spoke of these bright, energetic entrepreneurs who give themselves, without reservation, to their enterprise. "The newest hire is . . . forced to carry a Rugrats doll and order take-out Chinese food, the nightly company meal. 'How do you indoctrinate people into your culture? You baptize them,' Lui (the company founder) says. 'We want everybody to drink out of the same vat of Kool-Aid.'"[1] The church is that group of people who drink from the same vat and who have been immersed into Christ.

That same *Time* article about start-up companies in Silicon Valley states, "The labor market in the Valley is so tight that start-up CEOs spend most of their time recruiting. New entrepreneurs speak in religious tones about the importance of bringing in 'the A people,' of getting the right 'office mix,' about assembling 'the team.' (Typical usage: 'At the end of the day, it's not the business plan that matters. It's all about the team.')"[2]

The church is God's team, bound together by Christ's cord of love. Those who do not love Jesus also have their version of the church. It is a human need. Rarely do humans rejoice in complete isolation. There is a part of us that needs a group reality. As life goes on, that group becomes a center for us. For some it is the country club to which they go to play golf. For others it is the monthly fishing buddies gathering. For some it is the reading club that works its way through a juicy novel every four weeks. A motivated young entrepreneur spoke about how his business interests dictate his social life: "Dates bore me. Especially dates with women who aren't in the tech industry. That's my life. If they can't relate to that, then what do we have?"[3]

Do you hear the secular version of being equally yoked? Do you hear the nonchurch version of light connecting with light? In stanza three of Fawcett's hymn, the church is described as that gathering of people who share each other's woes. We also share each other's triumphs (Romans 12:15). That may mean rejoicing in another's business success, celebrating answered prayer or lingering at the bedside of a dying relative with our friends.

The background of "Blest Be the Tie That Binds" is a humbling reminder of what is important in life. John Fawcett (1740-1817) was a well-trained preacher and scholar who rejected many enticing offers to enter prominent arenas of ministry. He rejected those offers in favor of a small congregation in Wainsgate in northern England. He found himself bound to that body of believers and served there for more than fifty years. Ken Osbeck in his *101 Hymn Stories* says that Fawcett never earned more than $200 a year from that parish.[4] For Fawcett, experiencing the tie that binds was more important than material gain.

The late humorist Erma Bombeck titled one of her books *Family: The Ties That Bind . . . & Gag*. At times, the church is a tie that can bind and gag. But this I know: I am fuller, richer, deeper, more focused and more useful to God because I am a part of this mystical fellowship.

18

Soldiers of Christ, Arise

A CALL TO
APPROPRIATE MILITARISM

1. Soldiers of Christ, arise,
   And put your armor on,
   Strong in the strength which God supplies
   Through His eternal Son;
   Strong in the Lord of Hosts,
   And in His mighty power,
   Who in the strength of Jesus trusts
   Is more than conqueror.

2. Stand then in His great might,
   With all His strength endued,
   But take, to arm you for the fight,
   The panoply of God;
   That having all things done,
   And all your conflicts past,
   Ye may o'ercome through Christ alone
   And stand entire at last.

3. Leave no unguarded place,
   No weakness of the soul;
   Take every virtue, every grace,
   And fortify the whole.
   From strength to strength go on,
   Wrestle and fight and pray;
   Tread all the powers of darkness down,
   And win the well-fought day.

CHARLES WESLEY, 1749

$\mathcal{S}$oldiers of Christ, Arise" certainly is not a hymn that merely suggests or invites us to do anything. It commands us. It is a collection of staccato imperatives. Arise. Put your armor on. Stand. Take to yourselves the panoply. Go on. Wrestle. Fight. Pray. Tread. Win. Guard all your places. Fortify. Do you hear all those commands? This is not a writer trying to inspire the church. This is a general barking out orders. As politically incorrect as it sounds for us to imagine ourselves conquering another, we are indeed called to fight. The problem, however, is that it is a fight against the invisible. "For our struggle is not against flesh and blood, but . . . against the powers of this dark world and against the spiritual forces of evil in the heavenly realms" (Ephesians 6:12).

Many hymns allude to a warfare or militaristic stance. It is a fitting metaphor, given our struggle against the forces of evil. We sing "Stand Up, Stand Up for Jesus," along with "Onward, Christian Soldiers," "Lead On, O King Eternal," "He Who Would Valiant Be," "Am I a Soldier of the Cross?" and "Who Is on the Lord's Side?" In contemporary music, we sing Jamie Owens-Collins's "The Battle Belongs to the Lord" or V. Michael McKay's "The Battle Is the Lord's."

If we would be faithful disciples, we must never try to avoid the battle. Conflict is simply part of what it means to follow Jesus. That conflict is against the forces of darkness primarily, but it is a larger, more general conflict as well. Jesus said, "In this world you will have trouble" (John 16:33). As much as we might want to, we cannot avoid the prospect of warfare.

In fact, in the first chapter of his letter to the church at Philippi, Paul says that one of the ways an opponent will know we are followers of Christ is the way we face the foe (Philippians 1:27-28). The Bible knows nothing of a conflict between militarism and pacifism. It calls us to peace and warfare. We are to practice making and keeping peace with all humanity, while at the same time, being aggressive toward the forces and powers of evil. However, we must do spiritual battle with spiritual weaponry. The soldiers of Christ dare not fight the battle of God with the weaponry of this world. "For though we live in the world, we do not wage war as the world does. The weapons we fight with are not the weapons of the world. On the contrary, they have divine power to demolish strongholds. We demolish arguments and every pretension that sets itself up against the knowledge of God, and we take captive every thought to make it obedient to Christ" (2 Corinthians 10:3-5).

Were we to fight in our own strength and with our own weapons, we would be doomed. We stand in the strength of Christ. In him, we are not only victors now, but we are assured of ultimate victory later.

I have never served in the armed forces of my country, but I do know that a soldier is only as confident as the company that backs the soldier. It is the strength of numbers and the record of the corps in which one serves that give confidence. If I were a soldier, I would brag about my country's strength and my unit's skill. Only a fool would go to battle talking about personal prowess. When the soldiers of Christ land on the beaches of Satan, we dare not flash our insignias as if we in ourselves are mighty. If we are wise, we will point to our Commander and celebrate the strength of the unit—the church—of which we are a part. When this posture is ours, our enemies tremble. Our foes know their time is short when we proclaim the strength of our calling, sending, saving God. "He [the devil] is filled with fury, because he knows that his time is short" (Revelation 12:12). As we take seriously Wesley's admonition, we rise . . . and conquer.

19

We Gather Together

DARING TO APPROACH

1. We gather together to ask the Lord's blessing;
   He chastens and hastens His will to make known;
   The wicked oppressing now cease from distressing:
   Sing praises to His Name; He forgets not His own.

2. Beside us to guide us, our God with us joining,
   Ordaining, maintaining His kingdom divine;
   So from the beginning the fight we were winning:
   Thou, Lord, wast at our side: all glory be Thine!

3. We all do extol Thee, Thou Leader triumphant,
   And pray that Thou still our Defender wilt be.
   Let Thy congregation escape tribulation:
   Thy Name be ever praised! O Lord, make us free!

NETHERLANDS FOLK HYMN, 1597

$\mathcal{G}$ordon Cosby, founding pastor of Church of the Savior in Washington, D.C., had a speaking engagement at a church in New England. He found the worship experience dull and uninspiring. On their way back to Washington, he and his wife stopped for the night at an inn whose only available room was above the tavern. As the Cosbys heard the sounds from the floor below, they realized that the sounds of laughter and happiness were the sounds they should have experienced in church that morning. Gordon said, "I realized that there was more warmth and fellowship in that tavern than there was in the church. If Jesus of Nazareth had his choice he would probably have come to the tavern rather than to the church we visited."[1]

It is the dullness and lack of vitality in many worship experiences that discourage those who might attend. Their memory of the gathering of the faithful is not a pleasant one. Perhaps they were dragged to services by a well-intentioned grandparent. Maybe parents insisted their children attend Sunday services whether they benefited from them or not. Whatever the case, there are millions of people on the planet who would rather hang out in a tavern than gather with those who love God.

This hymn, which is most commonly sung at Thanksgiving services in the United States, is a hymn of gathering and thanks. Written in 1597 to celebrate a Dutch victory over the oppressive regime of Spain, the song has been attached to the story of pilgrim colonists who give thanks for the first bountiful harvest in the United States after their settling. One can see in the text the veiled references to things political. "The wicked oppressing now cease from distressing." "He forgets not His own." "So from the beginning the fight we were winning." "Thou, Lord, wast at our side." "Thou Leader triumphant." "And pray that Thou still our Defender will be." "O Lord, make us free." These are battles one could not have fought alone. The hymn is a reminder of the reality of corporate strength. No individual in the Netherlands could have withstood the power of Spain alone. When deliverance came, it was fitting that a gathering should take place. It is the collective "we" who give thanks to the God who has acted on their behalf. When the people speak, they acknowledge the ways of God. He hastens and chastens; he does what he does deliberately. He does not waver. He acts decisively. As he acts, he has an agenda, says this text. Some of what God does, he does in order to discipline his people. He chastens. The Scriptures teach that one of the purposes of suffering is that God might discipline us (Hebrews 12:6-7) and make his will known to us. If that be so, one can sing with gratitude of a God who chastens. While God is disciplining, however, he is also re-membering—he does not forget his own. In stanza one we sing of our gathering and of God's remembering. In stanza two we sing of God's presence with us. Note the vivid verbs: *guiding, joining, ordaining* and *maintaining.* The only fitting ending to such thoughts is "all glory be Thine!"

In stanza three the writer, speaking for the gathered people, says that all join in praising God, the triumphant Leader. While the con-gregation would like to avoid suffering if possible, they are nonethe-less prepared to praise God's name. This raising of the possibility of escape from tribulation reminds us of our Lord's request in the gar-den of Gethsemane. "My Father, if it is possible, may this cup be taken from me. Yet not as I will, but as you will" (Matthew 26:39). In that passage we see both the exploration of escape and the articula-tion of submission to God's sovereignty. The Bible is replete with re-minders of God's complete independence.

> *But he stands alone, and who can oppose him?*
> *He does whatever he pleases. (Job 23:13)*

> *Our God is in heaven;*
> *he does whatever pleases him. (Psalm 115:3)*

> The LORD *does whatever pleases him,*
> *in the heavens and on the earth,*
> *in the seas and all their depths.* (Psalm 135:6)

Often our skill and capability breed arrogance, and we forget that all we have is because of God. We gather together not to celebrate our accomplishments or to brag about the size of our budgets, our buildings or our mailing lists. We gather in order to ask our Lord's blessing and to celebrate his presence in us. It is God's maintaining and ordaining that prompts our praise. Gladly we submit to his reign and rule.

C. H. Spurgeon (1834-1892), one of Great Britain's most insightful preachers, said:

> There is no attribute more comforting to His children than that of God's sovereignty. Under the most adverse circumstances, in the most severe trials, they believe that sovereignty has ordained their afflictions, that sovereignty overrules them, and that sovereignty will sanctify them all. There is nothing for which the children ought to more earnestly contend to than the doctrine of their Master over all creation—the Kingship of God over all the works of His own hands—the Throne of God and His right to sit upon that throne . . . for it is God upon the Throne whom we trust.

Whenever we gather together to ask the Lord's blessing, it is with the understanding that this God may do whatsoever pleases him. It is within the confines of that acknowledgment of God's rule that we are ultimately free. Since the age of twelve, I have occasionally raised hamsters. I find this little rodent fascinating. My largest colony of the critters was twenty-six-strong. When I wanted to let a hamster out of its cage, but not have it run all over my house, I put it in an acrylic ball. Unscrewing the fun sphere, I'd place the hamster inside, reattach the two halves and place the ball on the floor. Because there were air holes all around the ball, the hamster was comfortable. The hamster inside the acrylic prison was both free and bound at the same time. The hamster could go anywhere the ball would take it, but the critter could not crawl under the refrigerator. Allow the analogy and picture us, lovers of God, as rolling around freely, but within the confines of God's sovereignty. We are bound but free. That liberation comes as we gather to affirm the Lord's being on our side. The last line of the hymn has the writer and singer crying out, "O Lord, make us free." That is what we all desire. We want to be free . . . and bound by this reigning God.

For All the Saints

A REMINDER ABOUT
OUR CURRENT STATUS

1. For all the saints, who from their labors rest,
   Who Thee by faith before the world confessed,
   Thy Name, O Jesus, be forever blessed.
   Alleluia, Alleluia!

2. Thou wast their Rock, their Fortress and their Might;
   Thou, Lord, their Captain in the well-fought fight;
   Thou, in the darkness drear, their one true Light.
   Alleluia, Alleluia!

3. For the Apostles' glorious company,
   Who bearing forth the Cross o'er land and sea,
   Shook all the mighty world, we sing to Thee:
   Alleluia, Alleluia!

4. For the Evangelists, by whose blest word,
   Like fourfold streams, the garden of the Lord,
   Is fair and fruitful, be Thy Name adored.
   Alleluia, Alleluia!

5. For Martyrs, who with rapture kindled eye,
   Saw the bright crown descending from the sky,
   And seeing, grasped it, Thee we glorify.
   Alleluia, Alleluia!

6. O blest communion, fellowship divine!
   We feebly struggle, they in glory shine;
   All are one in Thee, for all are Thine.
   Alleluia, Alleluia!

7. *O may Thy soldiers, faithful, true and bold,*
   Fight as the saints who nobly fought of old,
   And win with them the victor's crown of gold.
   Alleluia, Alleluia!

8. *And when the strife is fierce, the warfare long,*
   Steals on the ear the distant triumph song,
   And hearts are brave, again, and arms are strong.
   Alleluia, Alleluia!

9. *The golden evening brightens in the west;*
   Soon, soon to faithful warriors comes their rest;
   Sweet is the calm of paradise the blessed.
   Alleluia, Alleluia!

10. *But lo! there breaks a yet more glorious day;*
    The saints triumphant rise in bright array;
    The King of glory passes on His way.
    Alleluia, Alleluia!

11. *From earth's wide bounds, from ocean's farthest coast,*
    Through gates of pearl streams in the countless host,
    And singing to Father, Son and Holy Ghost:
    Alleluia, Alleluia!

    William H. How, 1864

*T*his text is a celebration of the hope and certainty we have as the people of God. I know some Christians who are terribly uncomfortable referring to themselves or any other living persons as saints. Yet the Bible uses that word freely to describe normal believers.

Through eleven stanzas Bishop How describes those who now rest from their labors and enjoy being part of the church triumphant, having passed through death. What is a saint? Who is a saint? Is it appropriate for us to describe ourselves as such? Before you read any further, let me answer the question: Yes! In the New Testament, saints were ordinary followers of Jesus. The Greek word for "saint(s)," *hagios*, is also translated "holy." The derivatives of that root are variously translated holiness, sanctified, sanctuary and holy place. When an article is holy, it is different.

The Old Testament speaks of the temple as the dwelling place of God. It was the holy temple because it was different from all other buildings. The Sabbath was to be a holy day, because it was a day different from other days. Moses was told to provide holy garments for his brother Aaron in order to give him dignity and honor (Exodus 28:2). The priestly clothes were to be different from his other clothes. God's name is holy, being different from all other names. It is fitting that we describe ourselves as holy, in that we strive to be distinctive in the world. In the best sense of the word, we are to be different. The reason God forbade marriage between Israelites and other nations is not because he is a racist; it is because he was eager for Israel to retain its sense of spiritual distinction (Deuteronomy 7:1-4; Ezra 10:10-12). When we make a commitment to live these distinctive lives without apology, we are right to call ourselves the saints.

This hymn was written as a tribute to all the saints who are deceased. However, many saints are still living. Michael Griffiths observes in his book *Cinderella with Amnesia* that while the word *saints* appears sixty-one times in the English New Testament, it appears only once in the singular[1] ("Greet every saint," Philippians 4:21 NRSV). Griffiths goes on to say that "the concept of a singular saint is foreign to the New Testament writers."[2] We are part of something much larger than our local congregation or our denomination or our county or our country. We are joined to the saints, both living and dead, by our commonly held profession of Jesus the Christ as our only Savior and Lord.

When Bishop How thought about those saints now asleep in death, he also thought about how God displayed himself to them. In stanza two, William How says God was a rock and fortress to those of old. That is, their strength and fierceness came from their God. In darkness he was light. In warfare, he was the captain. The church is that body of people who are engaged in a warfare posture all their days. From the time we say yes to Christ, we assume the posture of a soldier. In fact one generation of believers hands off the fight to another, and so the war between good and evil continues. So says stanza three.

As I take seriously the mandate to follow Jesus the Christ, I stand mystically with those who fought that same fight years ago. As Bishop How processes this thought, he concludes that one day this struggle shall end. What a reminder. We shall not eternally be in the fight. For us, the war lasts as long as life does. Then shall come what we sometimes simply call "The Day." At that point, all striving on our part ceases and we rest in him who is the Commander in Chief. In that day, the saints militant become the saints triumphant. In that day, we join those whose stories we've heard and whose songs we've sung. And who are these? They will be people from every tribe and tongue and nation. They will come, in the words of Bishop How, "from earth's wide bounds" and "from ocean's farthest coast." What a mission impetus. This hymn is often used at funerals. It would be equally compelling sung at missions festivals. We proclaim and labor in the name of Jesus so that people from every part of the globe may become saints.

I urge you to define and identify yourself not as an individual who will conquer all foes on your own—not even on your best day will you make your most significant contributions as an individual. See yourself, I implore you, as one of the saints. You are connected to something larger than yourself—the church. It does have its problems, imperfections and ills. But it also has its saints. And you are one of them.

Rescue the Perishing

A DUTY TOWARD
THE PRE-CHRISTIAN

1. Rescue the perishing,
   Care for the dying,
   Snatch them in pity from sin and the grave;
   Weep o'er the erring one,
   Lift up the fallen,
   Tell them of Jesus, the mighty to save.

Refrain:
   Rescue the perishing, Care for the dying;
   Jesus is merciful, Jesus will save.

2. Though they are slighting Him,
   Still He is waiting,
   Waiting the penitent child to receive;
   Plead with them earnestly,
   Plead with them gently,
   He will forgive if they only believe.

3. Down in the human heart,
   Crushed by the tempter,
   Feelings lie buried that grace can restore;
   Touched by a loving heart,
   Wakened by kindness,
   Chords that are broken will vibrate once more.

4. Rescue the perishing,
   Duty demands it;
   Strength for thy labor the Lord will provide;
   Back to the narrow way
   Patiently win them;
   Tell the poor wanderer a Savior has died.

FANNY CROSBY, 1869

$\mathcal{A}$s Christians we sure are an arrogant bunch, aren't we? We believe that all those who willingly reject Jesus the Christ are lost. In fact we would say that while they live they are dying. Isn't it judgmental and narrow to say others are "perishing"? They are entitled to their opinions and their views of things theological. How dare we suggest that our way is the only way?

Mission is a duty rather than an option. We are never to see the lost as those who have simply chosen something else. The Bible sees them as those who have not chosen Someone else; therein lies their problem. Our attitude toward them is to be one of compassion rather than pride or smugness or, worse, apathy. As insensitive as it sounds, those without Christ are spiritually dying. They are, in the words of stanza one, "the erring ones." Is Christ the only hope for these erring ones? Are there not other ways or other deliverers by whom they can be made right and whole?

The question that Crosby's hymn begs is whether or not we believe that John 14:6 is literally true: "I am the way and the truth and the life. No one comes to the Father except through me" (John 14:6). Perhaps Jesus does not mean what this appears to say. Maybe Jesus is simply stating his confidence in himself and offering himself, with exaggeration, as the most viable of all options. As comforting as that sounds, especially to those who are not willing to receive Jesus, it simply cannot be substantiated by the Scriptures. If the Scriptures are our authority for faith and practice, we must allow them to inform us. Besides John 14:6, which contains no permission for us to interpret it any other way than literally, the most compelling passage which speaks about and to the perishing is Romans 3:9-20:

What shall we conclude then? Are we any better? Not at all! We have already made the charge that Jews and Gentiles alike are all under sin. As it is written:

"There is no one righteous, not even one;
  there is no one who understands,
  no one who seeks God.
All have turned away,
  they have together become worthless;
there is no one who does good,
  not even one."
"Their throats are open graves;
  their tongues practice deceit."
"The poison of vipers is on their lips."
  "Their mouths are full of cursing and bitterness."
"Their feet are swift to shed blood;
  ruin and misery mark their ways,
and the way of peace they do not know."
  "There is no fear of God before their eyes."

Now we know that whatever the law says, it says to those who are under the law, so that every mouth may be silenced and the whole world held accountable to God. Therefore no one will be declared righteous in his sight by observing the law; rather, through the law we become conscious of sin.

From this passage we can observe four truths:

- All people, Jew and Gentile alike, are under sin (Romans 3:9).
- No Jew or Gentile was capable of pleasing God—no one was seen as righteous or good (Romans 3:10-12).
- It is to God that all must ultimately be accountable (Romans 3:19).

- Our keeping of the law cannot make us righteous. In fact, the law only makes us more conscious of our sin (Romans 3:20).

Our response to these truths ought to be an evangelistic and missiological one. Since these things are so, let us plead with people who have turned Christ away. Let us find winsome, creative, strategic ways to present Christ to the perishing. Let us care for the spiritually dying. I would be delighted if one could build one's own path to God and God deemed every path valid. That would give every religion, every cult, a warm fuzzy feeling that no matter what was preached or what people chose to believe we would all eventually go to heaven. Would that it were so, but it isn't. John Hick, who at one time was the Stuart Professor of Christian Philosophy at Cambridge University, said that different religions are "equals, though they each may have different emphases." A statement such as that would guarantee that you would be popular and nonoffensive whenever the subject of religion came up. What I wish or even believe has nothing to do with what is true!

Addressing an audience of three thousand at a congress of theologians, Cardinal Joseph Ratzinger said, "Today it has become a slogan of enormous repercussion to reject, as simultaneously simplistic and arrogant, all those who can be accused of believing that they 'possess' the truth. These people, it seems, are unable to dialogue; therefore, they cannot be taken seriously, because truth is not 'possessed' by anyone." The cardinal added, outlining the thesis of relativism, "We can only be in search of truth. However, against this affirmation one can object: What search is this about, if one can never arrive at the goal?"[1]

Both the Bible and this hymn make it clear that all are not spiritually equal. Some are lost, perishing, far from God. Perhaps this theological stand does smack of colonialism and smugness and even narrowness. The cardinal was right: there is no point in searching if ultimately you can never settle and say, "I have ended my search." Down in the human heart there is a buried feeling that only grace can restore. There is a receptacle that only grace can reach and awaken. Even if one were to concede that the Bible might be correct in calling us sinful and hopeless without Christ, it would seem that one would carefully, soberly explore the possibility of Christ's exclusivity. Crosby points us to the One who alone can save. It is because of his mercy that we are not consumed and it is because of our rebellion that we are often perishing. I called this chapter "A Duty Toward the Pre-Christian." Sometimes I use that phrase to remind myself that many to whom we declare Christ will receive him. I must believe that Jesus is merciful and that Jesus will save.

About Worship

O Come, All Ye Faithful

AN INVITATION
TO WORSHIP

1. O come, all ye faithful, joyful and triumphant,
   O come ye, O come ye, to Bethlehem.
   Come and behold Him, born the King of angels;

Refrain:
   O come, let us adore Him,
   O come, let us adore Him,
   O come, let us adore Him,
   Christ the Lord.

2. True God of true God, Light from Light Eternal,
   Lo, He shuns not the Virgin's womb;
   Son of the Father, begotten, not created;

3. Sing, choirs of angels, sing in exultation;
   O sing, all ye citizens of heaven above!
   Glory to God, all glory in the highest;

4. See how the shepherds, summoned to His cradle,
   Leaving their flocks, draw nigh to gaze;
   We too will thither bend our joyful footsteps;

5. Lo! Star-led chieftains, Magi, Christ adoring,
   Offer Him incense, gold, and myrrh;
   We to the Christ Child bring our hearts' oblations.

6. Child, for us sinners poor and in the manger,
   We would embrace Thee, with love and awe;
   Who would not love Thee, loving us so dearly?

7. Yea, Lord, we greet Thee, born this happy morning;
   Jesus, to Thee be glory given;
   Word of the Father, now in flesh appearing.

JOHN F. WADE, CIRCA 1743

$\mathcal{U}$nfortunately, we have a body of music that is only heard at certain times of the year. I say unfortunately because some songs are so rich that they deserve more regular exposure. Much music comes to mind as I write this: the John Philip Sousa marches that are played only on the Fourth of July at a patriotic parade or at a football game. There are the songs we sing only during Thanksgiving week (the fourth week of November in the United States). There are the performances of Handel's *Messiah* and Tchaikovsky's *Nutcracker* in December. There is the music of the Lenten and Passion seasons and the glorious music of Resurrection Day. Apart from a Christmas in July event, we only hear these pieces at the time of year for which they are held in reserve. In my concerts I play "Adeste Fideles" all through the year. Likewise, I don't let the time of year stop me from playing John Wesley's "Christ the Lord Is Risen Today." "O Come All Ye Faithful" is a song we hear and sing all too seldom because the calendar leads us to believe it would be inappropriate.

This hymn is a reminder to the people of God to present themselves before God in worship. We are to come in a specific way. We must not drag ourselves to a worship celebration. We must be marked, says stanza one, by joy and triumph. We approach the Christ child in order to see him. The text invites us to behold him who was born King. Whenever I hear a person coo over a newborn and say, "she's adorable" or "he's awesome," I want to intervene. I want to tell the person enjoying the child that no child is worthy of adoration or high honor except the Christ child. He alone is to be worshiped and adored. I have never told any human that I adore her or him. Nor shall I ever. Adoration is a posture reserved for God and God alone. It was appropriate that the Magi bowed when they saw the Christ child (Matthew 2:11). It is not appropriate for us to say to each other, "Oh, I adore you." The refrain of this hymn admonishes us toward a posture and a person. We are not to adore the idea of worship or a season. We are to adore a person.

Stanza two of the hymn, missing in some hymnals, is creedal in form, as it comments on the nature of Christ. It borrows language from the Nicene Creed.

We believe in one God,
the Father, the Almighty,
maker of heaven and earth,
of all that is, seen and unseen.

We believe in one Lord, Jesus Christ,
the only Son of God,
eternally begotten of the Father,
God from God, Light from Light,
true God from true God,
begotten, not made,
of one Being with the Father.
Through him all things were made.
For us and for our salvation
he came down from heaven:
by the power of the Holy Spirit
he became incarnate from the Virgin Mary,
and was made man.
For our sake he was crucified under Pontius Pilate;
he suffered death and was buried.
On the third day he rose again
in accordance with the Scriptures;
he ascended into heaven
and is seated at the right hand of the Father.
He will come again in glory to judge the living and the dead,
and his kingdom will have no end.

We believe in the Holy Spirit, the Lord, the giver of life,
who proceeds from the Father and the Son.
With the Father and the Son he is worshiped and glorified.
He has spoken through the Prophets.
We believe in one holy catholic and apostolic Church.
We acknowledge one baptism for the forgiveness of sins.
We look for the resurrection of the dead,
and the life of the world to come. Amen.

The early church used hymns to teach doctrine. We saw that when we looked at a text by Martin Luther. Likewise, here in this text John F. Wade teaches us about the nature of the Christ child.

Wade invites angels to join him as he exalts Christ. I can picture Wade enraptured by our Lord Christ, saying, "Angels, join me as I join you in praising Jesus." Wade speaks to the heavens. Whenever I sing this stanza, I am reminded of the nature of the church. We are an aggregation of people who agree that Jesus is to be adored. I sing with others and am reminded that I am not alone in my love of God, Christ and the Holy Spirit. I am joined by other mortals and the host of heaven. After a worship service in which I had preached about contentment, a parishioner asked me if we could practice our faith without dealing with people. I told her that would be impossible because of the nature of the church. The church is people, and our Papa God does his work through those same people. It is that engagement that keeps our faith from becoming abstract. While stanza two does encourage interaction with the citizens of heaven above, it keeps us firmly on the earth as we adore the Lord Christ.

The next three stanzas, which are not usually printed in North American hymnals, continue the thought of all creatures praising and adoring the Christ child. Shepherds, Magi and the rest of us are to bend the knee in worship. In fact, Wade finds it difficult to believe that anyone beholding the Christ would not love him. In the most evangelistic stanza of them all, Wade asks, "Who would not love Thee?"

Again pointing us to the nature of Christ, Wade's final stanza borrows language from the first chapter of John's Gospel: "The Word became flesh and made his dwelling among us" (John 1:14). In an old Syrian Jacobite prayer we read:

> It is very meet and right that we should give thanks unto thee; that we should adore, glorify, laud, exalt, honour, hymn with praises, bless and sanctify the one majesty of the Holy Trinity. . . . Not indeed that thy majesty requires our praise, nor that thou hast need of our thanksgiving. For those who praise thee are numberless; high authorities infinite, the clustering cherubim, thousands of bright seraphim and a countless host; multitudes and armies without number; ranks upon ranks of devouring flame; marvelous power of burning coal, legions which bear up the chariot of the cherubim, the revolutions of whose wheels are infinite; troops of seraphim which by the throb of their wings move the threshold; a shining galaxy which out of the midst of the burning coal is discerned by its own movements; thousand of thousands who stand before thee and myriad of myriads who praise thy being. And with one clear voice and one loving harmony, with sweet song and ethereal tongue, they cry the one to the other and raise their voices in eternal praise saying "Holy, holy holy."

What a rich expression this hymn is. It encourages pure, directed devotion. See the Christ; join others in bowing before him. Count him and only him as worthy of adoration. That sounds like an activity in which we might well be engaged all year.

It Is Well

SERVING GOD
EVEN THOUGH . . .

1. When peace, like a river, attendeth my way,
   When sorrows like sea billows roll;
   Whatever my lot, Thou hast taught me to say,
   "It is well, it is well with my soul."

Refrain:
   It is well (It is well)
   with my soul, (with my soul),
   It is well; it is well with my soul.

2. Though Satan should buffet, though trials should come,
   Let this blest assurance control,
   That Christ has regarded my helpless estate,
   And hath shed His own blood for my soul.

3. My sin—oh, the bliss of this glorious thought!
   My sin, not in part, but the whole,
   Is nailed to his cross, and I bear it no more,
   Praise the Lord, praise the Lord, O my soul!

4. And, Lord, haste the day when the faith shall be sight,
   The clouds be rolled back as a scroll;
   The trump shall resound and the Lord shall descend,
   "Even so"—it is well with my soul.

HORATIO G. SPAFFORD, 1873

$\mathcal{T}$he story of Horatio Spafford's personal tragedy that prompted the writing of this text is one of the best known in hymnody. Spafford was a Chicago-based businessman whose wife and four daughters preceded him on a boat trip to Great Britain. His daughters drowned at sea after the ship had been hit, but his wife survived the wreck. Spafford's hymn is a testimony to the keeping power of our God.

Someone has said that anybody who smiles when things go wrong is either a nitwit or an appliance repairperson. That person may also be a believer in the Christ, who is able to hold us together when we have been deeply hurt. Many people serve Christ and love him only when circumstances are very good. They love God in sunshine, but dodge the rain. Not Spafford. Did you hear that creedal statement? "Whatever my lot, Thou hast taught me to say it is well." This is the graduate level of the Christian faith, wherein we worship God even though the sea billows roll. This hymn shows us the difference between faith *as long as* and faith *even though*. Shallow believers love God as long as their family remains healthy, employed, well fed, clothed, intact and "successful." A maturing believer says, along with Job, "Though he slay me, yet will I trust in him" (Job 13:15 KJV).

When I sing Spafford's hymn, I use each stanza to remind myself of some lessons learned as I have grown in my faith. Let me offer these lessons to you so that a different perspective may be gained.

In our suffering, God will give us his words to sustain us. Spafford simply says, "Whatever my lot, Thou hast taught me to say." In all life's circumstances God has spoken and will continue to speak. This is the believers' confidence: God has spoken. This is the recurring refrain of the prophets of old. They did not merely preach what they wanted to preach; they had heard from God and prefaced their proclamations with "For the LORD has spoken" (Isaiah 1:2, 20; 40:5; Jeremiah 13:15).

In Jeremiah's day there was a strong tendency to believe false prophets' visions rather than believe the word of the Lord. The people of God were told to always seek to know what God said, rather than what any false prophet said:

> If a prophet or a priest or anyone else claims, "This is the oracle of the LORD," I will punish that man and his household. This is what each of you keeps on saying to his friend or relative: "What is the LORD's answer?" or "What has the LORD spoken?" But you must not mention "the oracle of the LORD" again, because every man's own word becomes his oracle and so you distort the words of the living God, the LORD Almighty, our God. This is what you keep saying to a prophet: "What is the LORD's answer to you?" or "What has the LORD spoken?" (Jeremiah 23:34-37)

For the prophet of God, the word from or of the Lord was primary. It was to be treasured above all. The people of God were to remind each other that God had spoken. In his hymn, Spafford reminds himself that the Lord of wind and sea had spoken and was teaching him something.

In our suffering, God will give us assurance that he is in control. I have always enjoyed the line in stanza two "let this blest assurance control"—may I be kept afloat by what I know to be true. May my blessed assurance serve me well and control me.

Shirley was a member of the church I pastored some years ago. Her husband had been ill a long time, and she'd had many sleepless nights as she took care of him. One morning she called my office and we chatted about the previous night. She said she had been up several times and thought she wouldn't be able to get back to sleep. "Then I remembered the words of the psalmist that God neither slumbers nor sleeps," she said. "I figured if God was up all night, I didn't need to be, so I went to sleep."

That's the privilege of every believer. We may rest in the Father's care of us. This assurance ought to comfort and control us. When the anonymous writer of the epistle to the Hebrews talks about the believer's privilege of access to God, the writer says, "Let us draw near to God with a sincere heart in full assurance of faith" (Hebrews 10:22).

Having assurance does not mean that we are arrogant. It means that we know that Christ has seen us and has regarded our helpless estate. Picture our Lord Christ looking in on us all the time. That's precisely what is happening. His eyes are fixed on us (Psalm 33:18-19). We speak anthropomorphically here, of course, of God and assign to him the attribute of a human being (*anthropos*). The truth is, he doesn't have eyes or lips or hands. But he does surely regard us—he looks on us with favor. It is this same blest assurance that Mary celebrated in the Magnificat, her song of praise. "My soul doth magnify the Lord, and my spirit hath rejoiced in God my Saviour. For he hath regarded the low estate of his handmaiden" (Luke 1:46-48 KJV). Spafford's second stanza seems to have been written with Mary's song in mind.

In our suffering, we are freed by the gift of God's Son. Spafford would have had reason to be anxious had he believed that his sin had only been paid in part by Christ. However, Spafford rejoiced that Christ had covered all sin. Consequently, Spafford no longer needs to carry it. Most of us can articulate the story of Christ's death, burial and resurrection quite well. Do we believe it? We need not bear our sins any more! Praise the Lord, praise the Lord, O my soul! When I have mused on our Lord's sacrifice on the cross, I have imagined a scenario in which I am standing beneath the cross, looking up at Jesus.

"You're perfect," I say.

He says, "Yes, I am."

"I'm not, am I?" I say.

He says, "No, you're not."

I say, "The Father is pleased with you, isn't he?"

"Yes, he is very pleased with me," he replies.

"You are full of righteousness, aren't you?"

"Yes, I am."

"And I am not, am I?"

"No, son, but you can be."

"But I'm full of sin."

"I know."

Then he looks at me and, with a twinkle in his eye and love in his heart, he says, "Want to trade?"

I look at him and, knowing he is serious, lay on him all my sin. He lays on me his righteousness. He who knew no sin became sin for me, so that I could know the righteousness of God the Father (2 Corinthians 5:21).

In our suffering, God gives his promise to encourage us. We who love Jesus and serve him as our only Lord are ridiculed often because of our faith. We are accused of being naive and shallow. It seems to me that it takes at least as much faith to reject the loving, living God as it takes to receive him. Yes, we believe much by faith and we are incapable of producing hard evidence for much of what sustains us, but a day is coming when faith shall be sight.

In the last paragraph of an essay titled "A Free Man's Worship," philosopher-mathematician-psychologist Bertrand Russell articulates the stance of one who has no certainty of that day when the faith shall be sight.

Brief and powerless is Man's life; on him and all his race the slow, sure doom falls pitiless and dark. Blind to good and evil, reckless of destruction, omnipotent matter rolls on its relentless way; for Man, condemned today to lose his dearest, tomorrow himself to pass through the gate of darkness, it remains only to cherish, ere yet the blow fall, the lofty thoughts that ennoble his little day; disdaining the coward terrors of the slave of fate, to worship at the shrine that his own hands have built; undismayed by the empire of chance, to preserve a mind free from the wanton tyranny that rules his outward life; proudly defiant of the irresistible forces that tolerate, for a moment, his knowledge and his condemnation, to sustain alone, a weary but unyielding Atlas, the world that his own ideals have fashioned despite the trampling march of unconscious power.[1]

Can you hear the hopelessness there? Even if that life to which we look is a myth, it has more hope in it than that. Because we have Christ's promise to return, we are not full of despair. Spafford's final stanza is a statement of brightness, predicated on the proclamations of the Scriptures. I am reminded of the many times our God gives us statements of bright hope.

> Paul, a servant of God and an apostle of Jesus Christ for the faith of God's elect and the knowledge of the truth that leads to godliness—a faith and knowledge resting on the hope of eternal life, which God, who does not lie, promised before the beginning of time. (Titus 1:1-2)

> We know that the whole creation has been groaning as in the pains of childbirth right up to the present time. Not only so, but we ourselves, who have the firstfruits of the Spirit, groan inwardly as we wait eagerly for our adoption as sons, the redemption of our bodies. For in this hope we were saved. But hope that is seen is no hope at all. Who hopes for what he already has? But if we hope for what we do not yet have, we wait for it patiently. (Romans 8:22-25)

> For everything that was written in the past was written to teach us, so that through endurance and the encouragement of the Scriptures we might have hope. (Romans 15:4)

Through him you believe in God, who raised him from the dead and glorified him, and so your faith and hope are in God. (1 Peter 1:21)

God is not unjust; he will not forget your work and the love you have shown him as you have helped his people and continue to help them. We want each of you to show this same diligence to the very end, in order to make your hope sure. We do not want you to become lazy, but to imitate those who through faith and patience inherit what has been promised. (Hebrews 6:10-12)

Like Spafford, we travel in hope, clinging to our Lord's rich promises.

Breathe on Me, Breath of God

CLAIMING THE
ENERGIZING WIND

1. *Breathe on me, Breath of God,*
   Fill me with life anew,
   That I may love what Thou dost love,
   And do what Thou wouldst do.

2. *Breathe on me, Breath of God,*
   Until my heart is pure,
   Until with Thee I will one will,
   To do and to endure.

3. *Breathe on me, Breath of God,*
   Blend all my soul with Thine,
   Until this earthly part of me
   Glows with Thy fire divine.

4. *Breathe on me, Breath of God,*
   So shall I never die,
   But live with Thee the perfect life
   Of Thine eternity.

EDWIN HATCH, 1878

*I*t has always disturbed me that the person of the Holy Spirit, who came to unite us, has become the focal point of many church disputes. This third person of the Trinity has been misunderstood in every age and in every expression of the Christian faith. Some traditions believe that when one comes to Jesus, one also receives the person and power of the Holy Spirit. Others believe that the salvation event is in two parts. According to this view, one receives Christ as Savior. Subsequent to that experience, the neophyte believer asks for and receives the Holy Spirit. That entrance of the Spirit may be accompanied by external demonstrations such as speaking in tongues. Others believe that the coming of the Spirit will be dramatic and memorable. Still others believe that the Spirit is a gentleman who quietly enters without a fuss. It is not my intent to write about the doctrine of the Holy Spirit in this chapter. Each tradition would surely agree that all followers of Jesus Christ need to be guided by and empowered by the Holy Spirit. In these pages I want to argue for the importance of a relationship with God the Father, God the Son and, especially, God the Holy Spirit.

We are unable to effectively live for Christ's glory without the energizing power of the Holy Spirit. The most common Greek word in the New Testament for "breath" is *pneuma,* from which we get the English word "pneumatic." A pneumatic tool is one that is powered by air or wind. Hatch's text is a prayer for the wind to blow on him. That's a mighty valid prayer, for we are not of much use to God in a non-pneumatic state. Depending on your position on the doctrine of the Holy Spirit, you could argue with the very first line of Hatch's text. Once we receive Christ, some say that there is no need to ask him repeatedly to fill us. But doctrinal positions aside, let us all agree that we cannot live a Christly life apart from Christ's power. That power flows to us by the Holy Spirit's invisible ministry in us.

Hatch's first stanza speaks of conformity. He admits that we cannot even love what Christ loves or do what Christ would do apart from the Spirit. Jesus said that when the Spirit came, he would teach the disciples all things and remind them of what Jesus said (John 14:26). If our goal is to be conformed to the image of Christ (Romans 8:29), then our cooperation with the One who conforms us—the Spirit—is critical. When old deacons used to pray in our worship services, I remember them praying that the Lord would "visit us this morning, for we can't do nothing 'til you come." That's what the first stanza says. We cannot operate in spiritual power until the wind of God blows on us.

In his account of the postresurrection appearance of Jesus, John tells us that Jesus commissioned his followers to go into the world. "'As the Father has sent me, I am sending you.' And with that he breathed on them and said, 'Receive the Holy Spirit'" (John 20:21-22). We cannot have an effective witness on this earth without the breath of God.

One of my son's playmates is a small boy who weighs less than most of his peers. On a windy day he accompanied us to a friend's house. On the way into the house he got knocked over by the wind. Within seconds he was on his back on the front lawn. Chuckling, I asked what happened. He simply said, "The wind." When you and I have a significant ministry and people inquire as to the source of our effectiveness, we may simply say, "The wind." This song is a prayer we need to pray often.

The breath of God affects our behavior. It also ought to affect our motives, so in stanza two, Hatch prays that God's breath would blow until it accomplishes the purification of the heart. Purity of heart is not merely thinking holy thoughts. To have a pure heart is to have one's very thought life aligned with God. In the words of stanza two, we pray for our wills to be at one with God's. This is no small request. It presupposes a willingness to give up my base desires for that which

most honors God. When this prayer is fulfilled, we want what God
wants. His desire is our desire. His thoughts are our thoughts.

> Will is the whole man active. I cannot give up my will; I must
> exercise it. I must will to obey. When God gives a command or
> a vision of truth, it is never a question of what he will do, but
> what we will do. To be successful in God's work is to fall in line
> with His will and to do it His way. All that is pleasing to Him is
> a success.[1]

What makes this difficult is that we have so much we want to do.
Our agenda sometimes conflicts with God's agenda. Rather than argue with the Eternal, we say, "Let my will be lost in Thine," to quote
another hymn ("I Am Thine, O Lord"). In *The Great Divorce*, C. S.
Lewis writes, "There are only two kinds of people in the end: those
who say to God, 'Thy will be done,' and those to whom God says, in
the end, 'Thy will be done.'"[2] Human willfulness directly opposes
God and his will for us. We ask, in this hymn, that the wind of God
would blow until we stop fighting God.

Earlier in this chapter I referred to the many positions on exactly
how and when one receives the Holy Spirit. A further part of that discussion has to do with how often one asks for his power. Do we pray
only once to be filled with the Holy Spirit? Or do we daily ask God
to fill us? I suggest that it is both, rather than either-or. At the point
of my receiving Jesus as Savior, I receive the Holy Spirit. Daily, I want
the Spirit to know that I intend to cooperate with him as he conforms
me to the image of Jesus. Some say there is one filling of the Holy
Spirit and many renewals. Others say we are filled one time and that
is sufficient. But let's not lose sight of the main point here: we need
the wind of God. We need it every minute of every day. So we are
praying that the breath of God does its work:

- until we love what God loves

- until we do what God would do
- until our hearts are pure
- until our wills are aligned with God's
- until the earthly part of us glows with divine fire
- until we live the perfect life of God's eternity

William Wordsworth wrote a poem in which he ponders humanity's willfulness and the wind of sorrow, which blows on us.

Weak Is the Will of Man, His Judgment Blind

"WEAK is the will of Man, his judgment blind;
Remembrance persecutes, and Hope betrays;
Heavy is woe;—and joy, for human-kind,
A mournful thing, so transient is the blaze!"
Thus might 'he' paint our lot of mortal days
Who wants the glorious faculty assigned
To elevate the more-than-reasoning Mind,
And colour life's dark cloud with orient rays.
Imagination is that sacred power,
Imagination lofty and refined;
'Tis hers to pluck the amaranthine Flower
Of Faith, and round the Sufferer's temples bind
Wreaths that endure affliction's heaviest shower,
And do not shrink from sorrow's keenest wind.

Do you desire the perfect life? So do I. Surely this is not possible . . . unless the wind blows.

Angels We Have Heard on High

A SONG FOR
ALL SEASONS

1. *Angels we have heard on high,*
   Sweetly singing o'er the plains,
   And the mountains in reply
   Echo back their joyous strains.

Refrain:
   Gloria, in excelsis Deo,
   Gloria, in excelsis Deo.

2. *Shepherds, why this jubilee?*
   Why your joyous strains prolong?
   What the gladsome tidings be,
   Which inspire your heavenly song?

3. *Come to Bethlehem and see*
   Him whose birth the angels sing;
   Come, adore on bended knee,
   Christ the Lord, the newborn King.

4. *See Him in a manger laid,*
   Whom the choirs of angels praise;
   Mary, Joseph, lend your aid,
   While our hearts in love we raise.

TRADITIONAL FRENCH CAROL
("LES ANGES DANS NOS CAMPAGNES")
TRANSLATED FROM FRENCH TO ENGLISH BY
JAMES CHADWICK (1813-1882)

$\mathcal{I}$n the late 1980s and the 1990s angels were extremely popular in North America. Television shows such as *Highway to Heaven* and *Touched by an Angel* all focused on the activity of angels in the lives of people on earth. Yet I am not sure most people could say they have heard angels sing. If we did admit to such an experience, we'd most likely do so in a very small circle of friends.

Angels protect (Psalm 34:7), they serve us (Hebrews 1:14), and they comfort us with good news (Luke 1:26-31; 2:9-12; Acts 27:13-26). They also sing (Revelation 5:11-12; 7:11-12). Having never heard one sing, I cannot vouch for the sweetness of their tone, but I do savor the imagery of stanza one of this hymn: "Sweetly singing o'er the plains" suggests a song that is pastoral and even antiphonal, as the mountains echo in reply. What are they singing?

"Glory to God in the highest." What a simple yet provocative song. The angels do not merely want God to be acknowledged. Rather, they want highest praises to go to this God. What does it mean to give God glory? The most common word for glory in the Hebrew language is *kabod*. Its root means "heavy" or "weighty." In contemporary language we might say a certain celebrity is a heavy-weight in his field or that an actress is a heavy hitter, turning out significant films year after year. To give God glory is to announce his heaviness. It is to live in such a way as to point people to the weightiness of the one true God.

Glory is always connected with radiance. We speak of a glorious, sunny day. We speak of heaven as the place of glory. The psalmist says that the created order demonstrates the glory of God (Psalm 19:1). In the New Testament, the Greek word for glory has to do with having a good opinion of someone or some object. It became attached to the concept of fame. One of whom we have a high opinion becomes well known. When God is exalted, he is raised up and made famous. To glorify God is to put his reputation before our own.

> Lord, I have heard of your **fame**;
>   I stand in awe of your deeds, O Lord.
> Renew them in our day,
>   in our time make them known;
>   in wrath remember mercy. (Habakkuk 3:2, emphasis mine)

God, in fact, jealously guards his glory and will not share it with any other. One of the most compelling proofs of the deity of Christ is that in him and on him we see the glory of God (John 1:14). God will not give his glory to another, yet his glory rests clearly on Christ. Therefore, Christ must not be another but God himself:

> See, I have refined you, though not as silver;
>   I have tested you in the furnace of affliction.
> For my own sake, for my own sake, I do this.
>   How can I let myself be defamed?
>   I will not yield my glory to another. (Isaiah 48:10-11)

The angels sing for God's glory. Their goal is not to attract attention to themselves. Rather, they are emissaries who aid us in seeing God shine. When the shepherds saw what God was doing at Bethlehem, they were ecstatic, and according to the second stanza, their joyous song was sustained. In Luke 2:9 we are told that the shepherds not only heard from angels that night, but that the glory of God shone around them. When they see and hear the angelic message, proclaiming the weight and radiance and fame of God seemed the most natural response. This good news cannot possibly be kept secret. The shepherds are compelled to engage others in acts of adoration. Stanza three urges, "come to Bethlehem and see"—exactly what the shepherds did on that night. They went to Bethlehem themselves, to see this sight of which they'd heard (Luke 2:15). After they saw the

Christ child, they spread the word concerning what had been told to them (Luke 2:17). All year that's what we are aiming for. We are to find winsome, creative, strategic ways to get women and men, girls and boys, to "come to Bethlehem and see, him whose birth the angels sing." We are to urge people whom God created to "come adore on bended knee, Christ the Lord, the newborn king." Ministry that is vital is a glad cooperation with God regarding the making of his character and his deeds known.

The idea of invitation permeates this Christmas carol. Not only do the angels and the shepherds get to join in the praise; Mary and Joseph are admonished to join in as well. Think with me about the physical setting that inspires this song. Mary and Joseph have recently been through the ordeal of childbirth. They are exhausted. If anyone had justifiable cause not to join in the singing at the manger, they did. However, the carol does not allow even the parents the option of not singing. Let all creation sing glory to God. Let all who understand the impact of this event sing glory to God. You, Mary, who have recently been through labor, lend your aid. You, Joseph, still confused about what all this means, lend your aid.

Larry Richards, in his *Expository Dictionary of Bible Words*, closes his article on "Glory" with these thoughts:

> The world is impressed by appearances. Wealth and position are equated with glory, and fame—the admiration of others—is eagerly sought. The Christian has a different set of values. To the believer, true glory is found only in the splendor of God. It is recognized as his character is displayed in his actions, and as it is reflected back to him as praise. We say with the psalmist David: "You are a shield around me, O Lord; you bestow glory on me and lift up my head" (Ps. 3:3). We glorify God by recognizing his presence in his actions and by offering him our praise. And we glorify God by being channels through which

the Holy Spirit, who lives within us, can communicate God to
those whose lives we touch.[1]

The highest praise be to the highest God!
Gloria in excelsis deo.

Epilogue

ON THE PLAYING,
SINGING AND PLACE OF HYMNS

*T*here is no halfway point with hymns. Either a congregation sings them well or they don't. Many people who are sure they don't like hymns have probably never heard one sung well. I maintain there is still great hope for those of us who like the sound of a hymn. The average hymnal has more than five hundred hymns in it. Yet the average congregation probably sings fifty to sixty hymns. They simply recycle the ones that are familiar, singing them with frequency. When one inquires about expanding the roster of familiar hymns, one is told something like, "Well, the congregation doesn't sing that one well. They really like #47."

How do we recover or discover the power of hymns in worship?

Affirm their value as a component of worship. When I was a college pastor, students would sometimes ask me, "Are we singing praise songs today or hymns?" That question suggests that hymns cannot be songs of praise. However, when sung well, hymns can usher us into the presence of Papa God. If we are to see hymns regain a place of usefulness in worship, we must believe such hymns are valuable, serve a purpose and are relevant. A friend of mine with teenage children said that when his children were in difficult spots and talked about how they coped with their problems, they more often than not quoted old hymns as their inspiration. My friend was surprised that they did not turn to newer songs. Hymns are valuable and sustain us in difficult times.

Make it known that you are committed for the long term. If you want to lead the discovery of hymns in worship, you will encounter opposition. Note I did not say you might encounter it. The easiest thing to do is back down when a complaint comes your way. Churches are often market-driven. If our customer base does not like our product, we are tempted to discontinue offering that product. Plan to forge ahead, offering hymns because you know hymns are part of a well-planned liturgical diet. Over the course of three to five years of singing hymns in one congregation, you will see significant results. Don't give up after three months. Give it three years, and then make an evaluation. Spiritual renewal is not for those who can only endure opposition for ninety days.

Inform the musicians that hymns deserve high energy. To my dismay I have noticed that some praise teams sing contemporary choruses with great enthusiasm and then change their countenance when they sing a hymn. Hymns should not be given less energy. That's a blatant case of age discrimination, wherein we favor the new and merely endure the old. Along these lines, commit to singing the entire hymn just as we would sing the entire contemporary chorus. I was in a worship service in which the leader said, "Let's sing stanzas 1, 3 and 4 of number 456." At the conclusion of the service I asked him why he omitted the second stanza. He said he did not know why he did. It was a habit. He also interrupted the flow of the hymn text. The easiest statement to make to a congregation is that we will give them what they want. The kindest thing to say to a congregation is that we love you too much to rob you of the pleasure of learning and singing hymns.

Expect the best from those who sing. When I was a pastor, the running joke among the people I served was that I would almost always stop the singing of a hymn. They were right. I was more concerned about our singing well to our God than I was about how people might perceive me as a worship leader. I expected our people to sing well. Some people sing poorly in worship, and no one stops them or holds them accountable for such poor investment of themselves. I would rather stop them and tell them that what they offered was not, in my opinion, worthy of them. They began to know that what they sang before God was to be of high caliber. God was expecting that, and so was I. What would happen to our congregations if we who led them simply refused to stand for poor performance?

Let the accompanists sound a clear sound. Have you ever heard an introduction that left you confused? Let us play in such a way as to make it very clear what is being played and when you are to commence your singing. A few lush chords and a gradual slide into a song may be the norm for singing a chorus, but a hymn needs a more pronounced beginning. Let those who accompany, play a recognizable introduction. There is no standard way to do this. Some play through the entire hymn, especially if it is new to the congregation. Others play the first and last lines of the hymn, giving a congregation a reminder of how the hymn begins and how it ends.

See hymns as part of liturgical literacy. There are several traditional pieces of worship order to which every worshiper should be exposed. A few examples are the Lord's Prayer, Psalm 23, the Apostles' Creed, the Doxology[1] and the *Gloria Patri*.[2] Imagine that over a period of years you offer a curriculum to those for whom you plan and lead worship. The curriculum would include songs, spoken pieces, Scripture passages and excerpts from the writings of church history. When people leave that sphere of influence they should be able to sing the songs, recite the creeds and offer the prayers.

Some years ago a preacher ended a service at which I was present by singing without accompaniment "My Jesus, I Love Thee." On the second phrase he asked the congregation to join him. Most people in the congregation did not know the hymn. When the service was over, a man in his thirties asked the minister of music, "Was I supposed to know that song the preacher was singing?" The minister of music replied, "Yes, and I'm sorry." The preacher assumed that this common song was known by all. The minister of music failed his congregant by not exposing him to such a song.

When children go to kindergarten, it is assumed they have learned colors, shapes, numbers and letters. Those elements and others form the common literacy expectation for kindergarten. The same applies to worship. See hymns as part of that which one should know. Ideally, we should be able to go to any worship celebration and have something in common with worshipers from other places.

When I was a pastor, I frequently introduced a new hymn each month. The choir would learn it in advance and then we would teach it on the first Sunday of the month. We sang that particular hymn each Sunday of that month. By the second Sunday the congregation was more comfortable and by the last Sunday of the month they owned the song. That plan would give a congregation twelve new hymns each year. I liken this to planning a diet for children. Knowing that children do not know what they need, parents choose the food. On their own, children would choose pizza, ice cream and other foods that might not constitute a balanced, nutritious meal. In worship, many congregations do not know what constitutes a balanced liturgical meal. So we plan for them. We put elements in front of them that they would not choose on their own. It is part of our gift to them.

John Wesley, in one of his hymnals, suggested some rules for singing hymns. They seem as fresh today as when they were written more than 250 years ago.

1. Learn these tunes before you learn any others; afterwards learn as many as you please.

2. Sing them exactly as they are printed here, without altering or mending them at all; and if you have learned to sing them otherwise, unlearn it as soon as you can.

3. Sing all. See that you join with the congregation as frequently as you can. Let not a slight degree of weakness or weariness hinder you. If it is a cross to you, take it up, and you will find it a blessing.

4. Sing lustily and with a good courage. Beware of singing as if you were half dead, or half asleep; but lift up your voice with strength. Be no more afraid of your voice now, nor more ashamed of its being heard, than when you sung the songs of Satan.

5. Sing modestly. Do not bawl, so as to be heard above or distinct from the rest of the congregation, that you may not destroy harmony, but strive to unite your voices together, so as to make one clear, melodious sound.

6. Sing in time. Whatever time is sung be sure to keep with it. Do not run before nor stay behind it; but attend close to the leading voices, and move therewith as exactly as you can; and take care not to sing too slow. This drawling way naturally steals on all who are lazy; and it is high time to drive it out from us, and sing all our tunes just as quick as we did at first.

7. Above all, sing spiritually. Have an eye to God in every word you sing. Aim at pleasing him more than yourself or any other creature. In order to do this attend strictly to the sense of what you sing, and see that your heart is not carried away with the sound, but offered to God continually; so shall your singing be such as the Lord will approve here, and reward you when he cometh in the clouds of heaven.[3]

If we would do what Wesley admonishes, how sweet will be the sound.

Notes

Chapter 1: Come, Thou Fount of Every Blessing
[1]Kenneth W. Osbeck, *101 Hymn Stories* (Grand Rapids: Kregel, 1982), p. 52.

Chapter 7: Great Is Thy Faithfulness
[1]Robert Murray M'Cheyne, "The Faithfulness of God," posted on Sovereign Grace Articles <http://sovereign-grace.com/379.htm>.
[2]A. W. Pink, *The Attributes of God* (Swengel, Penn.: Bible Truth Depot, 1961).
[3]J. Kirk Johnston, *Why Christians Sin* (Grand Rapids: Discovery House, 1992), pp. 39-41.

Chapter 8: O Come, O Come, Emmanuel
[1]Stephen Blank, "The Condition for US-Russian Partnership," *Orbis* 46, no. 4 (2000): 661-78.

Chapter 9: And Can It Be?
[1]Jac J. Muller, *The Epistles of Paul to the Philippians and to Philemon* (Grand Rapids: Eerdmans, 1955), p. 82.

Chapter 10: Amazing Grace
[1]Paul P. Enns, *Moody Handbook of Theology* (Chicago: Moody Press, 1989).
[2]Lawrence O. Richards, *Expository Dictionary of Bible Words* (Grand Rapids: Zondervan, 1985), p. 320.

Chapter 11: All Hail the Power of Jesus' Name
[1]John MacArthur, *Christ Humbled, Christ Exalted,* study guide (Chicago: Moody Press, 1990), p. 44.

Chapter 13: In the Garden
[1]James Sire, *Habits of the Mind* (Downers Grove, Ill.: InterVarsity Press, 2000), p. 205.
[2]George W. Sanville, *Forty Gospel Hymn Stories* (Winona Lake, Ind.: Rodeheaver-Hall-Mack, 1943).

Chapter 14: In the Cross of Christ I Glory
[1]James Denny, *The Death of Christ*, ed. R. V. G. Tasker (1902; reprint, Carol Stream, Ill.: Tyndale House, 1951), p. 235.
[2]John R.W. Stott, *The Cross of Christ* (Downers Grove, Ill.: InterVarsity Press, 1986), p. 296.

Chapter 17: Blest Be the Tie That Binds
[1]Romesh Ratnesar and Joel Stein, "This Week's Model," *Time,* September 27, 1999, p. 72.
[2]Ibid., p. 73.
[3]Ibid., p. 77.
[4]Ken Osbeck, *101 Hymn Stories* (Grand Rapids: Kregel, 1982), pp. 45-46.

Chapter 19: We Gather Together
[1]Elizabeth O'Connor, *Call to Commitment* (New York: Harper & Row, 1963), p.109.

Chapter 20: For All the Saints
[1]Michael Griffiths, *Cinderella with Amnesia* (Downers Grove, Ill.: InterVarsity Press, 1975).
[2]Ibid.

Chapter 21: Rescue the Perishing
[1]Cardinal Joseph Ratzinger, "Is It Arrogant to Say Christ Is the Only Savior? Asks Cardinal Ratzinger," (an address to theologians at the Catholic University of St. Anthony, Murcia, Spain, November 30, 2002), available at <www.catholic.org/cathcom/worldnews.php?ID=501# complete_story>.

Chapter 23: It Is Well
[1]Bertrand Russell, "A Free Man's Worship," quoted in the *Independent Review,* 1903.

Chapter 24: Breathe on Me, Breath of God
[1]Henrietta Mears, quoted in "Dream Big: The Hentrietta Mears Story," *Christianity Today,* June 21, 1993, p. 41.
[2]C. S. Lewis, *The Great Divorce* (New York: Simon & Schuster, 1996).

Chapter 25: Angels We Have Heard on High
[1]Lawrence O. Richards, *Expository Dictionary of Bible Words* (Grand Rapids: Zondervan, 1985), p. 312.

Epilogue
[1]Praise God from whom all blessings flow.
 Praise Him all creatures here below.
 Praise Him above, ye heavenly host;
 Praise Father, Son and Holy Ghost. Amen.
[2]Glory be to the Father, and to the Son, and to the Holy Ghost. As it was in the beginning is now and ever shall be, world without end. Amen, Amen.
[3]John Wesley, *Select Hymns.*

For more information about the
ministry of Richard Allen Farmer, visit:

www.richardallenfarmer.com